Refuge in the Shadows

Searching for Caring Community in the Midst of Trauma

One Woman's Journey
as a Mother and a Teacher

Kaisu Aldom

Refuge in the Shadows

tellwell

Tellwell Talent
www.tellwell.ca

ISBN
978-0-2288-3372-7 (Hardcover)
978-0-2288-3371-0 (Paperback)
978-0-2288-3373-4 (eBook)

Dedication

To my husband Dana and our five precious kids,

I'm so thankful we get to journey this life together

Table of Contents

Thank You

Dana – You are a man of deep compassion, strength and humility. You are someone who demonstrates steadfast love to everyone in your family each and every day. How lucky am I to be married to you and to get to journey through this life together? It hasn't been easy, and we've had to walk through more than our share of loss, pain and sorrow, but we've had each other, and for that, I am so grateful.

My precious children – My hopes for you are pretty simple: that you could rest assured in the love of the Father, that you would use your gifts to love and to serve others, and that you would find communities that would truly accept you, support you, and walk alongside you. I hope you know how incredibly proud I am of each and every one of you, and how thankful I am to get to be called your Mom.

My friends – *you know who you are.* Thank you for reaching out and persistently staying by the side of our family through all the turmoil and extra hard challenge from *this past year.* Thank you for wrapping your arms around our family (literally) with love and care — I am truly blessed to call you *friends*.

To my incredibly gifted, wonderfully talented and most gentle friend anyone could ever ask for, **Laurel Sprenger.** Some friends feel like sisters, and I'm so thankful you are one of them. **Your gift of art for the**

front cover of this book is precious beyond words. With much love!

Leanne Stam – Your background knowledge in trauma, in writing, editing as well as in education, helped to confirm that you were the person I needed to complete this project. Thank you for all of your encouragement and work on my manuscript. I look forward to sitting down for many more cups of tea with you in the future!

To my dear family Henni, Miika, Maria, Paivi and Hannu – I am truly thankful for all the ways we have been knit close together, even if physical distance has spread us all over this world. Thank you for encouraging me to continue with my studies and for believing that I could do it.

Meagan VanDiermen – Where do I even begin? Meagan, you are an extremely wise woman, a caring professional, and an incredibly kind person. I don't know where our family would be without your expertise as well as your heart and compassion for vulnerable families. Thank you for everything you have done for us through your advocacy, and for also being a sounding board for me throughout this whole journey.

Dr. Erika Penner and Dr. Kelly Saran – Thank you for being the kind of people that all of us need in our lives. Thank you for taking pause and allowing our story to finally be heard. Your willingness to listen and to believe means more than we can put into words. We are truly grateful for your kind and compassionate care.

Dr. Sue Montabello – The sincerity and kindness you demonstrated as a teacher was one of the most beautiful examples I have ever seen. Being your student changed me. Thank you for believing that my story was worth sharing and helping me find a way to do it. **Dr. Michael Ling** Thank you for cheering me on and for helping me find reasons to share my story. **Tannyce and Karen** Thank you for being there as my critical and needed friends during that last year at SFU.

And to **my Abba, Father** thank you for allowing me to be called your own even through times of doubt, anger, fear, and desperation. *Thank you for sending people to help carry this load.* I take refuge in you.

Prologue

All I have left is my story

When everything is stripped away,
your ability to work,
your capacity to meet with others,
your capability to participate, and
your time as a student
has even come to an end,
you're still fighting exhaustion
working through turmoil
and coming to terms
with a future so completely unknown.

The reality also is
that the life that you live,
that which brought you here
in the first place,

just keeps moving on

with no regard or patience
for how you may feel,
or for that which life is demanding
of you even right now.

And all that I have left
to offer you
is my story.

To share what I've been through,
to share where I'm now,
to share the insecurities
as I try to find a way of
how
        to
                move forward.

But, I can't.
I'm stuck.
My thoughts are spinning
around the fact that:

all I have left is my story.

I cautiously release it
to people I know,
wondering who
will receive it with care,
hear what I'm saying and
what has been said,
responding with
kindness, acknowledgement
and comfort.

Not everyone will,
but you move on,

knowing there is always risk involved
in sharing your story.

I think I'm ready to take that chance as
there's a burning in my soul,
an urgency
and relentless
tugging at my heart.

It's time.

It's time to
release those suffocating
hands of silence
that barred
me from speaking
and kept me hostage for all these years.

It's time to release my story.

It's all I have left.
It's all I can offer.

Please handle with care,
and allow my words to speak to you
as I tell you about my journey.
My voice
needs a place to be heard,
and my heart won't rest
until I've found a way
to share my story.
(K. Aldom)

The Clown

A delivery man is dressed up as a clown.
He stands in the lobby of a five-star hotel
waiting to deliver whatever it is
he has been hired to do.

Little does he know that
right before his eyes,
a child is about to be handed over
from one universe to another.
Safety with familiar people,
suddenly ripped out of their reach forever.

This child is three years old.
This child is being asked to put their trust
in complete strangers.
Am I going with the clown
or with the other two?
It is not a circus,
but the system sure feels like one.

Here are your new parents.
We know you've never met them before today.
It's ok,
their paperwork says they're fine.

After an hour, maybe two,
we are walking away.
Our backs turned to those the child knew,

our child reaching out and screaming
to be handed back to the safety
of the ones that have cared for them
since their time together began.

Suddenly, we are now a new family.
This child is wanted.
This child has been longed for.
Prayed over.
Dreamt about.
Already loved.
Promised.
Paper ready.
Soul in transition.
And yet as an adoptive parent,
I am part of this system too.
The one that permanently
removes a child from
everything they have ever known.

I'm pretty sure,
the clown is the only one left laughing.
(K. Aldom)

Adoption. A word that represents such dichotomies.

Loss - gain. Sorrow - joy. Separation - unification. Dread - excitement. Unknowns - reality.

We were prepared. We had read, listened, discussed, researched, attended workshops, joined groups, and done our homework. But then there was *trauma*. The word that changes safe to insecure. The word that throws everything you thought you knew out the window. Trauma from institutional care: seconds, minutes, days, weeks, months, years of one's childhood living in an institution where people are paid to meet a minimal level of your needs. A childhood spent away from loved ones. Complications from significant medical challenges met with harshness or left to be dealt with alone.

You look trauma in the eyes. It stares back at you in bewilderment, anguish, confusion, defiance, anger, sorrow, sadness, rage, and sometimes with no expression at all. This is my story of trying to find caring community while staring into the eyes of trauma, and it glaring back at me.

My Journey as a Parent

How will we get paid?

"How will we get paid
for the care of this child?"
This the greeting
I received
at my doctor's office
that one exhausting day in May.

Not a "Hello, is this your new son?"
Not a "You're back!"
"How are you doing?"
Not a "He's so cute!" or
"So happy for you!"

No,
"How will we get paid for the
care of this child?
You know it took the doctor 12 months
to get reimbursed
for the care of the last one?"

I look down at my child,
and think of everything
we have been through
in the two short weeks
we have shared.
Emotions as high as Everest
sorrow as deep as the Pacific.

Precious, yet fragile,
moments in time.

We're finally home!
Beginning our journey.
Looking for compassion and care.
Screw you! You callous lady.
Screw you!
(K. Aldom)

I am a mother. The road to get here has not been easy. There were times in my life where I wasn't sure if I'd ever get to experience what parenting would be like. My husband and I now have five children. Each child welcomed into our family has been a miracle and an incredible gift, and yet every one of our children's story is also surrounded by heartache, loss, anticipation, waiting and wondering whether this child would be able to join us. Our family is like any family really: we play games, go for walks; there are both laughter and happy moments; the kids fight; the parents are tired and at times we snap; we juggle work, school and all kinds of activities. And then in other ways, I guess, our family is not your typical one. Some of our kids have joined us through adoption, several of our kids have some kind of special needs, and we are larger in numbers than many families today.

The story I am about to share with you is ***my*** story. I am a mother and an elementary school teacher. I am surrounded by children in every aspect of my life. I truly can't imagine my life without kids in it. But I am no saint—kids and noise drive me crazy at times, just like the next person. It's hard work spending all day managing behaviour, explaining things carefully, and constantly adjusting expectations so that children can handle the world we live in.

But back to my story, the story I am about to share with you. This is my story of trying to find caring community while juggling a world filled with children and the many demands that come through the challenges of loss, trauma, adoption, and complicated medical needs.

Bringing a child home from another part of the world is not a scenario that everyone in society approves of. However much you know this to be the reality, it is incredibly deflating to run into these attitudes portrayed by the very people you thought were going to be on your team.

Carving a legitimate place for my kids in society, where they would feel welcomed and accepted, quickly and sometimes not so quietly, became my mission. Acceptance, inclusion, voice and healing, these were the things I went on a mission for, knowing that if I didn't, no-one else would.

Along the way, we as a family, have come across all kinds of people and all kinds of attitudes. We have experienced loving acceptance, a desire to understand, to listen, to show empathy and to faithfully walk alongside us. Sadly, we have also experienced complete rejection, indifference, inability to have compassion, and pressure for us to just "deal with it." Both of these attitudes have been shown to us first-hand by medical professionals, teachers, administrators, people we thought were friends, sometimes even family, as well as, of course, by complete strangers too.

We have been deeply touched by those who have advocated for our kids and who have loved on them and cared for them, those who have taken the time to get to know them and to have compassion for their complex needs. At other times, we have come across those who seem bothered, almost annoyed that they are being asked to deal with, accommodate, or try to understand a family and children with needs that are so much more demanding than what their experience, expertise, or interest allows for.

Because my family is complicated and much of what we live with requires extra attention, my full-time job became the information gatherer and advocate. I became the person who tried to find services, support, and a welcoming space for all of my children.

Behaviour Assessment

So, they wanted to assess behaviour
to better prepare the school system,
they said.
I read through their assessment
as they described my child.

They missed everything about you.
They didn't *even mention*
that which actually mattered...

where you had come from,
what all you had lost,
how we were just beginning to get
to know each other.

They completely misinterpreted your behaviour
and viewed you from the lens of someone
who had lived the privilege of stability.

You were just trying to survive,
trying to show what a child
who had lost everything
was capable of doing.

I ripped up the assessment.
What a waste of time!
How upset this all made me feel—
anger, sadness, sorrow for you.

How will I now find the words to
explain how loss and trauma behave?
How can I help them see you through a lens
of compassion?
(K. Aldom)

Finding a place of understanding for my children, in all aspects of society, has been a journey filled with countless battles. Children who come with a history of trauma (and in our case children who have also been adopted) are dealing with loss so profound that those of us who haven't experienced it cannot know what it is like. It is easy to make assumptions.

Integrating our kids into school and having them understood by other professionals took more care and special instruction than would be needed with a typical child. As Andrea Chatwin (2018), an adoption trauma specialist describes, "One of the greatest barriers to offering the right kind of support and interventions for children with a history of trauma and loss is the misrepresentation of their presenting behaviours" (p.6).

If we are to be an inclusive society where differences are welcomed and where we want to promote acceptance, we need to acknowledge that sometimes it requires more work, more creativity, more patience and more understanding to meet the varied needs of the kids around us. "Rather than making it the responsibility of children and families to fit the 'program,' real inclusion starts from the experiences of the child and challenges society to provide a meaningful place for them" (Hanvey, 2002, p.7). A place that shows our children acceptance and respect. A place of dignity and compassion.

Craig (2016) explains, "children with trauma histories continue to perceive adults as untrustworthy and the world as unfair" (p. 34).

Regaining that trust with adults takes time and nurturing experiences in which adults once again prove to be trustworthy, consistent, sensitive and attuned.

Sometimes, we also have to understand that what we might see as a simple expectation can trigger children with trauma in ways that are not logical. Judith Howard (2013) reminds us in her book *Distressed or Deliberately Defiant*, "those with poor attachment can have difficulty with emotional self-regulation and can very quickly become easily stressed and impulsive and/or aggressive when emotionally aroused" (p. 25). These are the times when professionals need to listen to parents, support them, and better educate themselves to understand what might be going on. It also requires humility to be open to the possibility that the expectations placed on a child or the way a professional is interacting with the child may, in itself, be triggering that child's behaviour, insecurities or need for special accommodations.

It is at times such as this, for example at school, at a dentist appointment, or a doctor's office, where parents need support, not judgment. Parents also need to be assured that those around them are willing to listen and to change their interactions or expectations so that the needs of their child are better met. As Chatwin explains, "If we are going to understand the experience of the hurt child fully, we first need to consider them in the context of their previous experiences" (p. 19). When deciding on needed services and support and when making plans for the child's future, taking those previous experiences into account is crucial to the well-being of the child.

Showing up

Do you know how much effort it takes
to just show up and to be here?
To have my child with me?
To convince them
that this appointment
is needed, that it
will be worthwhile,
will help
so that we can make a decision
about the next big thing?
That in the long run this
will make things...better?
I don't even dare to tell them
how I have my doubts and
how tired I am of this too.

I know
you don't want to miss
school again,
miss that special event,
miss that thing with friends,
miss that time to relax,
miss that time
just to be a kid.
I know.
It kills me too.

Instead, here we are **again.**
I dragged you in.
I brought you along and
you are expected
to sit
patiently, to
wait for hours
    yet again,
to be co-operative
to answer questions
to be talked about
as if you weren't even
in the room.
To be silent!
    yet again
    and again
    and again
    and again
(K. Aldom)

Draining

The non-stop complaints,
the expression that things just aren't
the way you wished
them to be,
the walking on eggshells
trying to ask for cooperation
or even some joy in our day.

Why is everything always so hard?
Can't walk
Don't want
Do I have to
Why now
Why this
How much longer
I don't want to
Why me
It hurts
It tastes bad
Why so early
Why so late
I'm tired
I'm hungry
I'm thirsty
Not now
Not later
Why not now
Why not later
Never!

It’s a nonstop juggling game
trying to find the compromise and a
way to just move on from the last thing,
take a step,
get ahead,
make progress.

But no…it’s exhausting.
these days of appointments and
trying to negotiate
every moment of our day

because it doesn’t make sense and
it isn’t fair
and *far too much* is expected of you.
(K. Aldom)

Memory Keeper

You know that photo you have of your child?
The one with them eating popsicles
and staining their toddler clothes?
Remember, that time they were learning to walk?
Do you have it on video?
What about their first Christmas?
Making funny faces at Auntie Linda?
Picking out a pumpkin at the patch?
Grama's 70th birthday?
Camping with the cousins?
Remember?

You talk about these events;
you laugh at the memories.
Family gatherings and your relatives reminisce.
You laugh, you smile.
Your child is part of the family.
They belong.
You hold their memories for them.
You've kept a stash for their wedding.
You know, you are building community.
You, the parent have an important role to play.

You are your child's memory keeper.

The camera, the video
all witnessing the change,
the growth, the humour, the cuteness.

The teacher asks you to think back to your childhood,
bring a cute baby photo,
tell your parents to share stories of you
when, if, that time.

Barren.
"Mom, help me!"

Hollow.
"I need to bring something!"

Desolate.
"Help me, Mom.
I need something.
Something. Something. Anything!"

Parched.
"Mom! Mom! Mom!"

I have failed.
I am so sorry.
There are no memories from your early years
for me to share.
(K. Aldom)

Outside the classroom door

School, a place for community and connection.
What happens when it is not found?
"My favourite subject is recess!"
Such a healthy and welcomed comment,
yet **you** whisper
it is your least favourite part of the day.

Alone.
Watching, walking,
waiting for connection,
community,
inclusion.

We say we are working on it,
yet there are children
outside every classroom window
never venturing any further
than the safety of the door.

What does inclusion mean
on the playground,
in the halls,
to those kids standing there,
each day
waiting to be seen
in plain sight,
waiting to be invited
to finally join in?
(K. Aldom)

I quickly came to realize that navigating society and navigating school were demanding enough, but navigating friendships for our kids was also met with challenges. As Judith Howard (2013) says, "children with poor attachment can have significant trouble trusting others and this can impact on relationships throughout their childhood, schooling years and adulthood" (p. 25). As healthy attachment is something that can take years to establish in an adoptive relationship, it was no wonder that forming friendships was often a deep struggle.

Rejection. The word that hurts more than any other. Rejection became a reality and part of our existence. Rejection on so many levels that at times it was hard to even breathe. As an adoptive Mom, I wanted nothing more than to demonstrate to my children that they were wanted, welcomed, and loved. But, what do you do when that message is called into question by the messages they are receiving from the world around them? When children call out differences, don't invite to play, and go out of their way to exclude?

"At-risk, adopted kids tend to absorb the message that they are unwelcome in this world. They easily feel unimportant, unworthy, and rejected "(Purvis, 2007, p.139). These are wounds that my children carry and scars that are not so easy to mend. First-hand experiences of witnessing rejection of my kids do something to you as a Mom.

It wasn't always just the kids. Sometimes it was the parental response to our children as well. Some parents were, and continue to be, quick to judge as they lacked the compassion to encourage their children to reach out, to welcome, and to foster acceptance and care. Other parents seemed to only see the bewildered survival behaviour and quickly made judgements based on that, taking no time to view our children ***as*** survivors who had been through experiences most of us would only read about.

Others were fascinated with the idea of adoption but made no effort to understand the impact of loss and trauma, nor to offer support when it was desperately needed. As Chatwin (2018) writes, "Adults often shy away from acknowledging a child's experience when it doesn't seem rational, logical or warranted" (p. 28).

Rude House Guest

Those are the words you used
to tell me how you perceived them.
You used so many more
hurtful descriptions,
callous, unkind, uninformed.
No compassion, no understanding,
no empathy.
You don't understand
the blank looks,
the non-committal answers,
the ways they just want to please.
You admit it too,
but how easily you
judge and tear apart
instead of seeking to understand.
You ask if other parents have
commented negatively on my child.
What are you insuniating?
Do you not see how
hurtful it is to be
throwing daggers
and tearing to shreds
an already broken soul?
You tell me you've been watching my child,
taking notes from a distance,
asking others what they've observed.
How is that kind?
You want me to know you

are praying for my child.
My child needs prayer in ***action:***
kindness, compassion,
inclusion, truth.
Could you try again?
(K. Aldom)

You signed up for this

I asked for
understanding and compassion,
and these were the words
you offered instead:

You signed up for this.

And yes, I did,
but did any of us know
what signing up to parent
was going to be like?
Could we have predicted
how hard it was going to be?

We need your support,
not your dismissal.
I signed up for this,
and I'd sign up again
with no hesitation.

But in the meantime,
I'd love for you to care enough,
to try to understand
this road is hard,
harder
than any of us could have imagined.
And we as a family have gained
incredibly much,

but our family's story is also
filled with deep sorrow and loss.

Our kids
didn't sign up for this.
They weren't asked.
They had no say.
And the loss they carry
is far greater than any of us
can understand.
I am here choosing every day
to try to help them make sense of that
and to find peace.
I chose this,
yes I did…
but this choice is not straightforward
and cannot be navigated
without support.
(K. Aldom)

The letter you never wrote

The one I've been waiting for:
to hear you say
how your heart hurts for us
because you are making the choice to enter
into our pain.

The one that acknowledges
how hard this is,
how I didn't choose this for me or my kids.
This isn't a choice
to go from one surgery to the next,
to have to battle medical needs
made so much bigger from the
entanglements of the emotional ones.
To never feel like
your head is above water,
to never know
what is around the corner.
No, I didn't choose this.
It just is,
and because it is

I need to hear you say:
I'm in this with you.
I am going to make the choice
to walk alongside you,
to listen,
to support,

to learn how to understand
and how to offer a practical hand!
I am going to help you see that
you are not alone!
(K. Aldom)

Trust was lost

Trust was lost
and we are living a reality
that we now can't share
with you.

Trust was lost
that you would respond
with care and compassion,
upholding dignity
and handling our reality
with words
that could have had
the opportunity to
soothe
and to heal.

Instead,
you've poured
acid into open wounds
and thrown
punches at
our broken bones.

Trust was lost,
and we wonder if it is
too late

for these souls

to be mended
by what was spoken
and communicated
by what was left unsaid.

Your opportunity
    Came,
        went,
            too late,

your missed opportunity
to be a part of
empathy
grace and
humanity.

Trust was broken,
and the question becomes
will there be another
moment in time
where trust-wounds could be healed?
(K. Aldom)

All of us are on journeys that are filled with challenges. That is what life is often like. A part of being human is going through difficult things. Our resources are limited and life is just busy, and as those of us with children know, it takes a lot of energy to raise kids. As I look back at our family's struggles and the battles we have fought, whether to find acceptance for our children, a place to voice our journey, or just plain simple care for our children's needs, it grieves my heart to acknowledge that even though we were surrounded by many types of community, we so often felt completely alone.

At times it seemed like every which way we turned, we had to explain, justify, and do more work than others to carve out a welcoming place for our family. The loneliness seemed to only grow. The more tired I became, and the more life demanded out of me, the less I was able to invite people into our world. Outings were often challenging because of the physical needs in our family. Schedules and parent-directed decision-making was important, as often this was our only way to keep our kids regulated and their environment somewhat predictable. All of these factors, however, contributed to our inability to participate in normal every day enjoyable things. At times this seemed to be hard for others to accept or understand, and they seemed to move on without us. Exhaustion slowly took over, and life switched from memory-making to pure survival, and then one day we looked around and realized that the invitations for us to join in with others were becoming more and more rare.

On feeling left behind

Do you ever get that feeling
that you were left behind?
Weren't invited?
Weren't encouraged to
join in?
Weren't asked?
You just weren't.

You watch the world go by.
You know it's still turning,

but your world has stopped,
frozen in survival,
every day filled with just trying

to make it to the end.

The carousel is moving.
People are getting on.
People are getting off.
There is laughter.
There is joy.

You see it,
but the sound never
reaches your ears because
you're just the distant spectator
that everyone left behind.
(K. Aldom)

"Darkness is not the whole of the story — every pilgrimage has passages of loveliness and joy — but it is the part of the story most often left untold. When we finally escape the darkness and stumble into the light, it is tempting to tell others that our hope never flagged, to deny those long nights we spent cowering in fear." (Palmer, 2000 p.18)

"It is now understood that working with people in trauma — hearing their stories of hardship and supporting their recovery — has far-reaching emotional effect on the provider." (Lander, 2018)

I lost myself

I lost myself,
and I don't know where to find me.
Somewhere along the way
I was gone.
All that was left
was a shell of a mom
going through the cycle
of need
unmet.
Bigger need
still not met.
Larger than life need
not possible.
Searching.
Searching.
Trying to be
a doctor,
a nurse,
a counsellor,
a therapist,
a specialist,
an expert.
An expert I have become,
but not the one
I had trained for.
I lost myself,
and somewhere I have gone.
I'm searching
to be found.
(K. Aldom)

The Battling Parent

This isn't who I am.
This isn't who I wanted to be,
but everywhere I look
there's a battle going on.

I'm so tired of fighting,
and just for once,
I'd love to be surprised
and for just *something*
to work out
without a dispute.

The endless explaining,
convincing
(not that we usually can),
Hoping, and praying,
that someone
would take us seriously
and take the lead of advocacy
on our behalf.

I'm so tired.
I'm so tired of fighting.
This isn't who I am
or who I wanted to be.

But if I don't,
and just let it go,

history shows
that harm will be done.

Yet the truth is,
that just for today,
    I have no fight left in me.
(K. Aldom)

Parenting children from difficult places is hard. My role as an advocate was important and needed, but it was not easy. I was an advocating mom trying to find a voice for my kids, a place for them in society, in our communities, amongst our friends, in our church, in school, and in our extended families.

Our children came home with many challenges and many complicated needs. My days were (more often than I care to remember) spent at meetings, consults, doctor's offices, therapy sessions, on the phone and computer, trying to make sense of and co-ordinate everything that was being said and planned for. Unlike a child born in Canada, my children had missed out on years of appropriate medical care. Unlike a child born into a family, my children had missed out on years of nurture and love.

So much of what we have been through is hard to even put into writing. What made everything even more challenging was that we weren't only trying to untangle loose from the trauma that our kids accumulated prior to adoption, but also the trauma load that kept on growing: experiences of rejection from those whom we had been counting on; feelings of being dismissed when trying to explain our kids; complete misunderstanding of our kids' behaviours; refusal to see their need for dignity to be upheld; difficult medical appointments, surgeries, and long complicated recoveries; and sadly also questions, doubts and dismissals of our concerns when we asked for more help, accommodations, support, or resources from health care and school professionals.

Our life turned into exhaustion from days at the hospital and the endless follow-up visits. I carried so much guilt from the constant poking and prodding, questions, and therapies that I had to put my kids through. I was weary from the false reassurances I was forced to continuously make that somehow there would be an end in sight to all of this. It wasn't just our kids with trauma stories that were suffering and exhausted, but the reality was that the stress of years of overwhelming demands and living in an environment that was filled with emotional volatility, was taking a toll on every single member of our family. We parents were exhausted, and at times emotionally unavailable and overstretched. Time and time again we needed to ask our older kids to take on far more responsibility than perhaps they should have at the ages that they did. With no grandparents, aunts, or uncles within two thousand miles, we needed full co-operation and lots of help from all of our children. What choice did we have?

Advocate

Contact. Meet with. Explain.
Testing. Opinions.
Research. Co-ordinate.
Pass the message.
Try to make sense of.
Differing perspectives.
Who do we trust?
Email. Research some more.
Phone call. Contact. Meet with.
Repeat.

Pharmacists.
Physiotherapists.
Orthotists.
Family doctors.
Counsellors.
Pediatricians.
Social workers.
Orthopedic surgeons.
Neurologists.
Occupational therapists.
X-Ray technicians.
MRI technicians.
Anesthesiologists.
Speech pathologists.
And so many many many more…

Teachers.
Educational assistants.
Special needs co-ordinators.
Learning assistance teachers.
Learning assistance co-ordinators.
Psychologists.
Administrators.

Contact. Explain. Meet with.
Research. Co-ordinate.
Advocate. Advocate some more.
Who do we trust?
Who do we feel safe with?
Who is listening
and hearing
what is being said?
Is there anyone who genuinely
cares and would be willing to
act?
Pass the message.
Try to make sense of it all.
Email. Phone call.
Repeat. Repeat. Repeat. Repeat.
(K. Aldom)

The little David

When you feel like David,
but there are no more rocks to throw,

your bag is empty,
and you aren't standing on a bank
of a river
but rather in 2019
on a slab of cement,

you see Goliath
sneering at you,
laughing,
peering down,
unrelenting
with a message
that is loud and clear:

"You're just the little guy
trying to fight a mighty battle.
Don't need to listen to you.
Whatcha gonna do?"

And too bad for me—
we seemed to have reached
the land of Goliath clones,
one dressed in a suit,
another wearing a white coat,
and yet another a casual friend.

My bag is empty.
I have no army to back me up.
It's going to take a miracle
for Goliath to have a change of heart.
(K. Aldom)

The Wizard

Sometimes it takes a journey
to find what you are looking for.

Tinman? Lion? Scarecrow? Wizard?
Who are you trying to be?

What if you tried
to put yourself in my child's shoes,
not the sparkly red ones
(those don't fit on everyone's feet),
but rather,
the worn, tattered, battered ones,
the ones they try to walk with
each and every day.

You seem so determined to be right,
to know what's best, to lay down the law,
and to immediately tell us
what your rules are.

And yet,
if for just
        one little moment,

you'd try to imagine what all this might feel like
for someone who walks this weary path
and carries the burdens of difference
every single day

perhaps then, you could see
how your power to do something
could be used
to make that path a little less
crooked, and maybe even a
lot more smooth.

I guess I have a wish for you
that one day,
maybe you could reach that place
where you realize that
being a powerful and scary wizard
isn't all it is cracked up to be
because guess what:
it takes courage to speak up for the voiceless
it takes wisdom to practice inclusion and
it takes heart to show some real compassion

and without courage, wisdom or a heart
you're just a wizard, a hollow façade.
(K. Aldom)

Deflated Balloon

There is no fight left in me tonight.
I'm a deflated balloon.

The courage I once felt
is gone.

Perseverance
that still lingered
has disappeared.

Hope
tiptoed
into the shadows.

I am now surrounded by
a mist of silence.

Fear, anxiety, anger, and sadness
have all been emotions
that I have carried for far too long.

Tonight, I feel nothing. I am numb
with an eerie oblivion
descending on my soul.

The battle is over;
there is no victory.
We have to walk away
and accept that we have lost.

We gave it our all.
We fought. We argued.
We tried. We advocated.
We rallied. We prayed.
But all in vain?

Not tonight,
but perhaps tomorrow,
I'll find what it takes to reach for the
pump, to pull out the patches
and to try to salvage
what's left of me.
(K. Aldom)

Is it over?

We wait.
We sit.
Hearts are racing.
We know what's coming.
There's no choice.
I wish it was me instead.

Is it over?
Yes, yes, for now it is.
There's more?
Yes, yes, I'm sorry there is.
For now, just rest,
don't worry,
just rest.
It hurts.
I'm sorry.
It hurts.

Screaming, exhaustion.
Loud cries, piercing,
the sounds reach every heart,
every soul.
You promised. You said.
I didn't know.
You promised. You said.
This wasn't the plan.

Can I see your eyes?

Look at me please.
Turn your head.
Can you hear me?

I need you to know I love you.
I am sorry.

Please, look at me.
Where have you gone?
(K. Aldom)

Those Eyes

You know those eyes
that you see on children,
when you take one look
at that picture on the news
or in a magazine?
You can see that the child
is completely shut down?
There is disaster all around her.
There is maybe war, extreme poverty,
an earthquake,
or some kind of extreme trauma,
loss or suffering.
You know those eyes that are hollow and
show no signs of life
even though they are still living?
Those eyes,
they captivate you.

I've held a child with those eyes.
I have looked into those eyes.
I have been there.
I have witnessed.
I have held that child.
I have offered comfort,
food, a drink, words, hugs.

No response.
Nothing.

I feel their breath,
I see the lungs moving up and down.
I feel the sweaty head,
the emotionally limp body.

It does something to you.
It changes you.
Your heart can barely stand it.
You are broken like
never before.
Waiting for life to re-appear
in those eyes
that belong to my child.
(K. Aldom)

The truth is, people only saw glimpses of our lives. We lived through hurried doctor's visits where our kids didn't have time to process or react. Our kids walked through school days in which they learned how to hold their emotions and hurts until they got home. We experienced time with friends who didn't see the consequences of a late night or the effort it took to even just get out the door. We muddled through situations where people chose to ignore boundaries that we had set, therefore sending mixed messages to our kids. We were then left to deal with all of the emotion that had to be processed and played out behind closed doors, out of the public eye. The details of what this was like have been shared with very few even though this heightened level of emotion, anguish, rage, and pain was part of our daily lives for many years, and continues to be so. No one in our family is immune to it. Behind closed doors, we as the parents are most often the recipients of everything our kids feel, while every person in our family is affected by these strong emotions.

Closed Doors

There is now a physical barrier
between myself and my child.
The sounds of exhaustion,
fury, and deep sorrow echo through our house.
Both sides of the door
stare at each other.
Hours have passed.
Words have been shared.
Rage, emotion so dense,
impossible to pierce.
Questions for which
I have no answers.
Hopelessness.
Not knowing what to do.
Comfort.
Rejection lingers.
Minutes, hours, days, weeks, months
have turned into years.
Behind closed doors, we try to seek help.
Professionals, appointments, articles,
advice, counselling, websites,
books, meetings, prayer.
We quietly tiptoe and try to open doors,
looking for answers, looking for hope.
Trauma.
A world we live behind closed doors.
(K. Aldom)

How are you?

How to even answer?
How to tell the truth?
"We're ok." "We're hanging in there."
Or would you like to know about the hell we've been through
and how we just got back again?
Do I share about the pain story,
the physical agony
of flesh poked, prodded, sliced, and cut?
Do I tell about the exhaustion
that has haunted me
on this relentless journey?
Of the needs too many
that I just don't even know how to carry?
Do I share the story of lived-trauma?
The ripping away and forever asking
for co-operation?
Do I speak out loud of the hurt,
of friends turning backs,
of physicians dismissing,
of family not reaching out in empathy,
of feeling at times so ***completely alone***?
"How are you?"
"No, really, how are you?"
Did you genuinely want to know?
(K. Aldom)

Extreme Parenting

Extreme parenting,
is what she called it.
A stranger and
Facebook friend,
she hit the nail on the head.
I'd never thought of it as such,
but extreme parenting
it is indeed.

Extreme in demands.
Extreme in expectations.
Extreme in needs.
Extreme in how tired
you end up feeling
and how extremely lonely
this has all become.

Thrill-seekers search
for extreme events.
Celebrity wannabes
use such for attention.
Some make a calculated choice
to participate,
others seek approval after
losing their privacy, dignity and
self-respect.

But, I am just a mom,
begging for my life to not
feel so very extreme
anymore.
(K. Aldom)

Acknowledgement

I googled the word acknowledgement,
and the google dictionary said:
"Acceptance of truth
or the existence of something."

The example from Oxford online
on how to describe this word
could not have just been a coincidence for me to find.

"There was no acknowledgement
of the family's trauma."

That about sums it up,
doesn't it?
Our truth.
My reality.
No acknowledgement of
how hard this has been.

I accept it.
I know this is what we are living,
but how do I find a way
now back on to my feet
when trauma,
whether acknowledged or not,
keeps on
shifting the narrative?

Like an earthquake
rocking our world
and making it impossible
to land on solid ground.
(K. Aldom)

A Mother's Heart

How much can a mother's heart hold?
How much
is truly required?
How many
memories of desperation
should a mother's heart
need to store?

How much can a mother witness?
How much
can a mother see?
How many
moments of anguish
should a mother's mind
need to ignore?

How much can a mother encourage?
How much
can she persuade?
How many
moments of negotiation
can this mother possibly
be responsible for?

How many a dream has been dreamt?
How many
a prayer was prayed?

How many times
have I pleaded
that this heart be
expanded some more?
(K. Aldom)

The aspect of our lives that seemed the hardest for me to come to terms with was how often I felt alone. Alone to carry these burdens. Alone to bear the weight. Even at times, while surrounded by people, I knew I was carrying a solitary silence of suffering that I was unable to explain and found too difficult to share.

What complicated this feeling of loneliness was that as a special needs and adoptive parent, I had to continuously make the call of how much of my children's stories and struggles was I willing to put out there? If I didn't, how could people understand? But if I did, would I be betraying my children's trust and need for privacy?

Navigating community and connection are not straightforward in the age we live in. We tend to hide behind polished stories on Facebook and Instagram. The words "How are you?" have shifted from being a question to a greeting, and seldom do we wait long enough to truly hear what another might answer to these words. It all weighed heavily on me, this lack of connection. I shared, but only so much. I sought help emotionally, but only so much. I put one foot in front of the other and just somehow kept going on. I longed so desperately for people to see and to notice (and was hurt when those close to us dismissed, seemed oblivious to, or rejected our pain), but I also doubted myself and often questioned if I just wasn't trying enough, doing enough, wasn't organized enough or working as hard as I should. But deep inside, I knew the realities of our life. I knew what we had lived through, and I knew that there was a reason I was in pain.

I know I am not enough

I know I am not enough
to meet the needs you have,
the hurt,
the pain,
the loss,
the fear,
the confusion,
the anger,
the anguish,
the upheaval.
I know I am not enough,
yet I am trying,
trying to be the sponge,
the one to soak it all up,
to hold it for you,
to manage it,
to make sense of it,
to carry it,
to ultimately wipe it away.

But, I know I am not enough.

The sponge is dripping.
It's wet and heavy.
It can't move.
It can't breathe.
It is only making a mess.

The sponge needs to be squeezed.
It hurts.
It can't hold any more.
But how, where, when?

I've reached my capacity.
There is no more room
for pain.
It is all spilling out.

I am drowning.
I am not enough,
and I am drowning.
(K. Aldom)

I wrote an email

I wrote an email
some years ago,
but it never did get sent.
I stumbled into my drafts tonight,
and there it was, waiting to be read.
The letter listed everything
we were going through
at the time:
crisis
exhaustion
withdrawal
isolation
neglect
emotions
institutionalization
trauma
therapies
endless research
chronic illness
challenge.
Hanging on

by
an
extremely
thin
thread.

Faking it,

too hard to share,
truth too painful to admit.
I wrote an email,
but never had the guts to send it,
not knowing how it would
have been received.
I soak in the words, and a
cloak of sadness descends on me.
Parts of this family's history
is painted in very dark colours,
camouflaged in darkness.

Not sent. Not received.
Reality locked in words
stuck behind a computer screen.
(K. Aldom)

I wish I could say that I had the courage to let people know how hard things were, but most often, I didn't give myself permission to do that. Our family walked through a fog of one crisis after another for a decade with those around us not paying enough attention and having very little idea of what we were going through. Some things seemed to get easier at times: we reorganized our schedules, we withdrew from many activities, and then we withdrew from some more. We changed churches in search of one that offered more support; we sought trauma counselling for our children; we tried to carve out time to go for yearly holidays; we re-organized our priorities, and we re-organized them again. I hung on to my career working the minimal possible amount (even though I loved my job and waited years on the sidelines hoping for our home life to settle so that I could work more days) all the while juggling what little time I had at work amid surgeries, endless appointments, and the many responsibilities of caring for a large family.

You carry

You carry
this knowledge
of another reality
deep in your soul,
not shared,
not publicly voiced.

Every once in a while,
you let another peek in.

Their reaction determines
whether to share some more:

the raised eyebrows,
the questioning,
the blame,
the eye rolls.

The knowledge
is a secret.
How long will it be hidden?
(K. Aldom)

Breathe

Just take a breath.
It's not so hard.
No more gulping air
into those lungs,
rather slowly,
slowly stretch and fill.
Shallow, shallow.
No capacity.
Flat.
Show me
how to breathe again.
Pitter patter,
feet on floor.
Questions.
Answers.
More and more.

Breathe.

Just breathe.

You can do this.

It's not so hard,
but why
does it take
all I've got
to move those muscles,

to flesh them out so far
and fill that lung mass
with life, with air,
with life-giving
capacity?
(K. Aldom)

More than I can handle

They say God won't give you
more than you can handle.
What an absolute lie
and a terrible joke.
This is more than I can handle,
more than I can deal with.
This is bigger and harder
and tougher and more complicated
than any heart can bear.

This is more than I can handle!
And God I need you.
I desperately need you
to take it on
because even if I can't handle it,
I want to trust that you will
send someone
to help carry this load.
(K. Aldom)

In the fall of 2016, I took a huge leap of faith and went back to being a student. My topic of study was inclusive education, and week after week, I realized how my personal experiences were interwoven into almost everything we discussed. Over the next two years, I immersed myself into learning everything I could about inclusion and becoming a society where all kids are welcome.

Along the way, while I researched about challenging behaviour, social-emotional learning, the effects of trauma, and the load that we carry as we care for hurt kids, I also read about the importance of self-care, and thought to myself, yes, that does sound very important. I studied about healthy classrooms and eventually started trying to put into place a trauma-informed practice at work. All of this helped, and I became so much more aware of the theory. I perhaps even parented better and became an even more caring teacher. But the truth is, it wasn't enough. I was learning lots of theory, I was applying new-found knowledge, but I was too overwhelmed to pay attention to everything that was going on with me.

Sometimes, all it takes is for one person to show you just a little bit of empathy for you to feel like you can keep going on, even for just a little while longer. As much as I had often felt through the years that the struggles of our family's life were mine alone to bear, I don't want to disregard those acts of kindness when someone noticed and paid attention to our needs: the friend who offered to take our kids while one was in surgery, the acquaintance who offered a hot meal and cared to ask how we were managing, the rare physician who seemed to reach my eyes with empathy and wanted to know how I was holding up, our life group at our new church that cared on us, the friend who faithfully checked in and offered her listening ear, or my parents and siblings that empathized from the other side of the world. All of these moments definitely encouraged me and gave me a bit more strength to carry on for a little while longer.

Hilde

I am sitting on my garage floor
surrounded by puddles of grief,
stress, and discomfort.
Screams fill the air,
echoing through space
that is seldom empty.
I've been here too many times before.

I try to get up and start cleaning,
but can't see in front of me;
my eyes are swollen and blurred.

I try to lift my child
out of this mess that unites the two of us,

but can't.
I'm unable to continue
as feelings of isolation, loneliness,
exhaustion, and complete failure
grip hold of my body.

How can I go on?
These long days of consults,
meetings,
appointments
come with many names.
Poking and prodding.
A child who is unable to handle

the expectations,
the pain, the reminders
of days past and present,

long days of sorrow
and anger,
compounded trauma
and feelings so big
that the body physically reacts,
dispelling its insides for the outside world to see.

Suddenly, I hear a small voice behind me
“Can I help?”
I am taken aback. Words my soul longs for
as I turn around
and see my elderly neighbour Hilde
is standing at the door, a grey-haired angel.
(K. Aldom)

Help me to let go

Help me to let go
of the bitterness
that stems from hurt.
I don't want to live
under this burden
any more.
Rejection.
Neglect.
Feeling
overlooked.
Unseen.
Not noticed.
It happened,
but help me to
move on
to find
healing,
to know that
some may have
chosen to ignore,
but not everyone did.
Help me to see
and to let go,
to move on,
to forgive.
(K. Aldom)

These offers of support helped me to take another step forward, but the truth was, the accumulation of so many years of compounded trauma and non-stop advocacy and battle had left me exhausted and barely hanging on.

For years on and off, I had been carrying with me (and trying hard to hide the symptoms of) secondary trauma, depression, anxiety, vicarious trauma and burnout such as "feeling diminished joy, feeling trapped, having feelings of hopelessness, heart palpitations, trouble sleeping, worrying, feeling impatient" (and the list goes on) (Kostelyk, 2018, p.29). If I am honest, these above-mentioned symptoms had been my constant companion for as long as I could remember. I had quietly shared these feelings with my spouse but had not admitted them to my closest friends or family. I struggled with the messages of "you chose this," and the feeling that surely *if* it was so bad, more people around me would notice, and do something about it: friends would include us, invite us into fellowship, reach out and offer to help in concrete ways. It seemed like I was always confused as to what it meant to truly be part of community. Did people know what was going on? Did they care?

There had been days when all I could do was cry, curled up in a ball, hiding in a closet. There were weeks where I didn't sleep through the night, and my heart only raced with anxiety. To be completely honest, it had been years since I had felt fully relaxed or rested (even while on a holiday). I was ashamed. I knew I was beyond exhausted, and in need of help, but I didn't know how to permit myself to rest or how to ask others to support me. I was from Finland and raised by Finnish parents, and even though I had lived in many parts of the world, only now have I started to realize how deeply ingrained on some very sad level is this need to demonstrate that I have *Sisu*[1] and a good old Protestant work ethic[2].

So, I continued to put one foot in front of the other, showing up to keep my commitments and all the balls in the air. I was used to working hard and having lots on my plate and had grown up in a family that modelled the importance of sacrifice. I also believed I had no choice if I was going to have any identity outside of being a medical caregiver and a relentless advocate for my kids. I needed to stay strong and to manage. If I wasn't going to, where would it leave my family?

And then one day, I guess I just couldn't do it anymore.

In the spring of 2019, in a matter of 24 hours, three different medical professionals told me something I did not want to hear. I was on the verge of complete collapse and that if something wasn't done, my health would not be able to sustain all that I was trying to carry. As these words were spoken to me, and as I allowed my realities to be voiced, in those

---

1 Sisu - a Finnish concept described as stoic determination, hardiness, grit and bravery (Wikipedia)

2 Protestant work ethic – a concept that emphasizes hard work and discipline (Wikipedia)

moments in the doctors' offices, the exhaustion from the past decade, the feelings of abandonment and loneliness, the feelings of complete despair and battle, the fatigue from advocacy, the unresolved mountain of trauma, the expectations I had placed on myself, and the commitments that I had taken on, all came crashing down and flooded over me like a tsunami.

I was burned out. I was completely done, and I had no option but to accept what was being said.

In the days, weeks and months that followed, as I submitted to my doctor's recommendation and accepted my need for a long term medical leave, I slowly realized that for the past decade I had been fooling myself to believe that all that was needed was for me to try harder. This was what I, at times, thought my faith was also calling me to do: to sacrifice, to serve, and to put the needs of everyone else before my own, even at the cost of my own health.

But as my world around me completely collapsed, and the weeks and months went on, I had to face the question of "How had I got this all so wrong?" During my studies about trauma, I had read endless pages about the need for self-care, the dangers of burnout, and about the warning signs of fatigue. But in some twisted way, I had internalized the thought that everyone around me deserved and needed care, but that somehow that same care didn't apply to me.

Permission never granted

The irony of it all:
I walk away from my doctor's office,
now the third medical professional
to look me in the eye
and to tell me:
I'm sorry,
but, you can't go on…

The words pound in my head:
burnout, exhaustion
How can this be?
I've been searching for healing
for everyone around me.
I've been looking for ways
to take care of others,
to advocate even when I have nothing left,
to build caring community for
my students,
my kids,
my spouse,
my friends.

But the reality hits me in the face.
My head knows the facts,
the urgent need for self-care
in the midst of it all,
but…
through it all

permission never granted
by this overachiever,
this perfectionist,
the one who comes from a line
of strong work ethic,
of relentless sacrifice,
this person who so desperately wants to
do it all well and then some,
to put into action the knowledge gained.

Too much to do.
Too much to accomplish.
Too much to juggle.
Too many to take care of.
No permission.
No time.
No energy.
No sleep.
        Exhaustion.

Just ignore.
Stuff it down.
Be brave.
Put on a smile.
Answer to others,
"I'm good."

And now the reality
has come,
the table has been turned.

I have nowhere to hide,
no options anymore.
They tell me I have to
STOP!

They tell me I need
to rest,
to unburden,
to work through
that which has been lived
in a hurry,
and that which was never
slowed down enough
to think through,
to process
and to come to
terms with.

That had been the plan
all along,
but the truth be told,
I never got around to it.

Permission never granted
for myself to take a rest,
to feel that which needed to be felt,
to share that which needed to be shared,
to be healed from that which needed healing.

So, here I am,
advocating for care

and neglecting to care for
the one who stands before you.

I hang my head in shame
and vibrate with feelings
of loss and anger.
Tears stream down my face.
I have failed,
oxygen mask left hanging
in mid-air.

I am an empty bucket
with nothing left to give,
but this time, the signs are there:
if I continue on,
I will shatter into pieces,
and there will be no more.

Am I relieved?
Is it good to be found out?
Was rest poured upon me?
The words my soul has been longing for,
hiding in the depths of my being
for too long to remember,
silently begging for someone to notice that
permission needed to be granted.

I don't know any more how to feel.
Exhaustion has been my best friend
through relentless years of

caring, advocating, researching, listening,
co-ordinating.
No time to pause, no time to take care of me.

I wrap myself in a blanket of sorrow and confusion,
hostility towards having to let go,
a body aching with burnout and exhaustion,
a heart bursting with emotion
but not knowing how to feel.
A road to healing must somehow
now be found.

Permission has been granted
for me to start receiving care
and to learn how to take care of me.
(K. Aldom)

"Self-care is never a selfish act – it is simply good stewardship of the only gift I have, the gift I was put on earth to offer to others. Anytime we can listen to true self and give it the care it requires, we do so not only for ourselves but for the many others whose lives we touch" (Palmer, 2000, p.31).

I look back at the last ten years of my life. What would have it looked like if I could have reached out for more help and if the communities I was a part of had reached out more to me? Do we dare to ask for care, or do we just busy ourselves trying to care for others? Why should we care about others? This was a question I had asked of so many. What does care look like from medical professionals, from teachers, from administrators, from our community groups, from our family and friends? How do we better educate others on the effects of trauma and how exhausting caring for the traumatized can be? How do we move forward in a society that forever calls us to be more and more self-reliant and inward focused?

How could have I communicated better my need for more help and support? Was the responsibility on us as a family to always be the ones reaching out? Our family was a part of a small close-knit community, in a church that we had been a part of for a decade through all three of our international adoptions. We had expressed several times how we were in crisis, but the truth was, we did not feel heard. When you are in the midst of it all, and you feel dismissed, I guess you just stop talking about it. You long for someone to notice and to offer some help. Isn't that what community is about? People noticing that you are falling apart and offering to do something about it?

Caring Community?

Every **Sunday** I hear from the pulpit
about the caring community that surrounds me.
I was up all night tending to the needs of many.
Jet-lagged, traumatized, we carry on.

Every **Monday** I watch and wait,
wondering when this community will arrive.
I was out all day looking for answers,
so many unknowns,
so many professionals to consult
and to hear from.

Every **Tuesday** I pray
that at least someone would come to the door.
I was at the computer in the midst of naps,
holding, rocking, praying,
trying to understand what all this will mean;
no-one has time to really explain.

Every **Wednesday** I listen
for footsteps to approach our home.
I was out all day again,
appointment number 11 this month,
all with a child scared,
wounded, and needing more than I can give.

Every **Thursday** I ponder
why the knock is not sounding as a greeting.

I was cleaning up, washing up,
trying to deal with the extra load,
cooking, organizing,
trying to find normalcy in utter chaos.

Every **Friday** I watch and wait,
thinking surely, they'll be here soon.
I was at appointments again,
dealing with situations that were
exhausting and stressful.
My child doesn't understand, won't co-operate.
It is all just too much…
each meeting meaning many more.

Every **Saturday** I begin to hurt.
All those times I showed up for you.
Where are you?

Where is my caring church family?
I was trying to juggle the needs of so many;
I lost myself along the way.

It's **Sunday,**
and you tell me again,
how fortunate we all are
to be in such caring community.
(K. Aldom)

The Other World

Care to enter another world,
one that's dark and messy?
Just warning you that in this world,
it is bound to be uncomfortable,
and you might feel something
that you didn't want to receive.

No expectations!
And I understand
if you choose not to enter in.

It would take time.
It would take effort.
And it may even take
a whole lot of patience
and a lot of
sitting in silence
and listening hard.

To enter in, you would need to let go
of answers,
of being right
and of that which
is easy,
that which can be laughed off,
joked about,
treated lightly,

Or made to seem
like not such a big deal.

So, if that's what you're looking for,
please don't come in.
don't even peek around the corner.

This place isn't for looky-loos,
those that are curious
or those that want to know
for the sake of having something
to tell the next person.

No, the other world
is a fragile place—
one filled with people who are broken,
those who are lost,
those who have been hurt,
and even
those who aren't sure
how to find their way out.

This may seem too heavy.
This may seem too hard.
And it is.
That's why most
don't choose to come here.

But it is comforting to know that
God holds the other world,

and those that are in it
close to His own heart.

And every once in a while
He sends a special someone over
to reassure those of us
who are living there
that we are not alone.
(K. Aldom)

The Tsunami

The enormity of the past ten years is
like a tsunami slowly making its way towards me.

I see it creeping on the horizon,
and at times think I must be dreaming,
imagining it,
and even if it is there, I think,

if I keep running,

surely, I won't get caught in its path.

But others voice they see it too,
and honestly from their
perspective, it is much bigger
than I even realize.

There is nowhere for me to hide.

Time has run out for me to get out of its way.

I have no option,
but to turn around and face it.
The wave crashes into me,
and I know I am at its mercy.

Take me wherever you may.

No option left
but to battle through it
and to, hopefully, one day,
land on the other side
where dry ground can be found again.
(K. Aldom)

Some might read my story and wonder why I hadn't actively done more to care for myself. Maybe the thought is that I took on too much and deserved the load I was carrying. The ideas around self-care and community care have been on my mind lately. I had read several books and articles over the years that reminded me of the importance of self-care. I knew that "on a basic physiological level, parents need to replenish themselves. It's essential for the entire family's well-being. Without refilling your own bucket, you can't effectively offer healing to your children" (Purvis, 2007, p.231). I knew this to be true. I knew the importance of eating healthy, exercising, and getting enough sleep. I knew I was supposed to be taking better care of myself. But the reality was, *I wasn't able to*. My trauma burden and my level of exhaustion had grown so large that it had paralyzed me. I was so wrapped up in caring for others, I just didn't know how or have the energy to also be caring for myself.

I recently found the following quote, "Shouting 'self-care' to people who actually need 'community care' is how we fail people" (Nakita Valerio), and it struck a nerve with me. Looking back at the past ten years, I am starting to think that as important as self-care is, caring for ourselves takes us only so far. With all the reading I have done, I have concluded that what we need *more* than anything else is community care. We need to go back to the idea that "it takes a village to raise a child" and the Cree belief that "every child needs many mothers" (Brendtro, 40). We need each other; we need community. We need to feel cared for by others, and my family and I need care too!

"Yes, we are created in and for community, to be there, in love, for one another. But community cuts both ways: when we reach the limits of our own capacity to love, community means trusting that someone else will be available to the person in need" (Palmer, 2000, p. 48).

As I think through the past ten years of my life, the struggles, the joys, and all of the demands that have been placed on me, I speak with confidence in saying that all along the way, it would have made such a big difference for me and my family if caring community had consistently gathered around us. If more people around us—whether they were medical professionals, teachers, administrators, friends, neighbours, relatives, church members, or family, whichever community we belonged to—if more of these people would have taken the time to notice, to ask and to really listen, to practice compassionate empathy and to be willing to learn and to enter into our pain, I truly believe it would have changed the narrative of this story.

"If you somehow spot someone trying to conceal their pain, if you see their body crying out so loud that symptoms are hard to hide, if you see them unable to make sense of those symptoms, please offer your help to them. It can be as simple as asking them how they feel, if they would like to talk about it. Invite them over for something simple and safe like a coffee, but don't be offended if they don't take your offer straight away. Just state that you are here for them and make sure that they understood your will to listen. But don't ignore their pain." (M. Paccard, 2018)

As I am slowly beginning to understand where healing comes from, my ideas around what caring community is all about are beginning to form. What I am proposing is that healing can be found in environments where we feel safe, in situations where we feel we can trust, in relationships that we believe are filled with compassion and empathy. Healing can be found in places where we are given a voice, where we are free to express all of our emotions without judgement, and where people take the time to hear our struggles and to acknowledge them. These are the steps towards healing that I am discovering and that I now know I need to find a way to share.

Throughout all of my personal struggles, I was also walking on another path. This path was intrinsically intertwined with my journey. My journey as a teacher needs to be told separately to be fully understood. Therefore, I will put my own trauma journey on hold and share what was happening for me as a classroom teacher.

My Journey as a Teacher

I welcome you here

I stand at the door
to welcome you here.
Let this be a place
of refuge
for the anxious,
the angry,
the joyful,
the tired,
the confident,
the scared.
Come, join us in community
with those that can offer you
friendship,
understanding,
and a place to just rest.
Everyone is welcome here!
Everyone belongs.
We will walk this road together.
You are not alone.
(K. Aldom)

"We must hold to live life fully and well, the deeper our faith, the more doubt we must endure; the deeper our hope the more prone we are to despair; the deeper our love, the more grief we are likely to know"

Parker Palmer, 2003, from "Teaching with Heart and Soul"

What is happening in my classroom?

I had been teaching for close to two decades when I was given the chance to dig deep into my practice through a university graduate diploma program. Being able to step back, observe, take notes, and find out what your students were doing was an incredible gift.

I was working in a school in Surrey, B.C., Canada with a population that was mostly made up of first and second generation immigrant families. The school community thrived on relationships, however, what I came to discover was that loneliness was also a part of many students' lives. I was teaching part-time in two different job share positions, both in intermediate (4-7) grades. Our school population was made up of children from diverse ethnic backgrounds and different economic stabilities.

In the first year of my graduate studies, I ended up working with a group of students that was very receptive to a more open-ended way of learning. I thoroughly enjoyed experimenting with new ideas around writing, through differentiated instruction as well as developing tasks that integrated multiple intelligences. I gave my students lots of choices that year, and they expressed excitement towards learning that I had not seen for a long time. As I entered the following year of work, I was eager to continue with my learning journey and to further my discoveries.

However, the year that followed was very different. Both of the classes I was teaching in that fall happened to be filled with behaviour that was disruptive, needy, and very difficult to manage. With one of my classes, we worked through our issues, and the students eventually settled down. But the other class stood out, and in my two-decade teaching career, I'm not sure I had ever felt so discouraged. In this class, we seemed to have ended up with so many students with difficult behaviours that getting through just a regular day was almost impossible.

As the year progressed, I became increasingly frustrated with my efforts to give students independence and choice. Time and time again my attempts to make learning fun and interesting seemed to be sabotaged by the same students which resulted in the whole class joining in the chaos. After weeks of spending more time on classroom management than actually accomplishing anything, I finally decided that I had no choice but to withdraw the plans I had made, take a step back, and re-evaluate what I was trying to do. I was feeling very disheartened by the thought of going back to more teacher-directed learning, as it also seemed to be the only method that was keeping my students safe and engaged.

At a school-based team meeting that fall, a group of us teachers and other support staff were discussing some of the challenges in my room. We talked about the same reality that all schools are facing with support services spread thin across multiple classrooms. When some of the creative solutions to try to meet all of the students' needs were further talked about, our district psychologist spoke up. She encouraged those of us in the room to consider things from a different perspective. What she suggested was that the solutions and supports that we were looking for might, at least to some degree, be met through the students themselves. Our district psychologist basically said that more help is not coming. We are overstretched and underfunded as a system, and while we fight for more support and funding for our kids, in the meantime, we need to start being more creative in the ways we find support for our students and their many behavioural and unmet emotional needs.

As discouraging on many levels as this is to accept (and it really shouldn't be this way, but that is a whole other research topic), I was very intrigued by this idea and decided that day that what our psychologist was suggesting was something I needed to look into. So, after talking with her some more through emails and a few meetings, upon her suggestion, I ran a sociogram with my class. Through this tool, I was to try to find out who in my class were the students needing the most emotional support and who of my students might be the ones willing and able to offer some help.

Doing this simple activity changed everything for me. I didn't realize it at the time, but it was the beginning of my journey into a search to find caring community.

Wanting to find out the Why

Increasingly, over the past two decades as a teacher, I had been finding that more and more students entering my care were anxious, defiant, stressed, uncooperative, fearful, having trouble with relationships, at times uninterested in school, disruptive, attention-seeking, careless, unmotivated, and so on. Kids just overall seemed less settled. I also felt that as a teacher, behaviour issues were often taking over our ability as a class to learn.

I wanted to find out why, and I wanted to make the changes needed so that our days weren't always only focused on behaviour. So, this began a new journey for me: setting aside all other priorities in my room and finding out the *why* and the *story* behind the behaviours I was seeing.

During the following weeks, I thought to myself, what better way to do this then to ask my students to share more about their lives? Over the course of my third and final field study for my GDE (Graduate Diploma of Education), I decided to develop a program that would focus solely on building classroom community, teaching kids about empathy, and giving students a place and a voice to share their stories. From there, we would take it wherever it needed to go.

Over the next several months, I put all other learning on the backburner and systematically introduced activities that I had either found or created myself that would allow this process to happen. Along the way, I kept a close record of what I was observing and what I saw as important to notice. I asked my students a lot of questions and had them fill out reflective responses after each activity so they could process what they were feeling and so I could find out what was happening in their hearts and minds as we walked through these different tasks.

I was not prepared for what started to take place. In a matter of weeks, the flood gates started to open, and I suddenly learned more about my students than I had ever had the privilege of learning in my whole career.

I quickly found out that students were longing to share their stories and that they were telling me things that were burdening their hearts. I learned about fears, failures, relationship problems at home as well as with friends. My students shared about things that were hard for them, things that had traumatized them, as well as things that made them feel angry, sad and alone.

Over the course of the year, I became the story keeper of so many of my students' stories. The deeper we got into our SEL (Social Emotional Learning) unit, the more students wanted to share. I also realized that some of my students' stories needed far more extensive support than I had to offer. So, I started having regular conversations with the school counsellor, the administrators, the social worker, the support workers as well as both of my job share partners. We contacted parents, set up counselling sessions, and worked with the students trying to meet their expressed needs. I was often told that year how amazing it was that students were opening up to me at this level. I thought so too. But of course, as the person who was on the front line collecting all of this information and making decisions on how to respond, I was also well aware that at times this was a heavy experience for me to walk through. I was mindful of the fact that "in a school community, finding those that are available to support your work is important" (Jennings, 2019, p.117). However, as a very part-time teacher, juggling two different classes of students, it was sometimes hard for me to navigate and to figure out what that meant for me.

Equipped with this new-found knowledge and coming to the realization of how needed a focus on social-emotional learning had been, I applied and got accepted into a Masters program. I had learned over this very emotional year with my energetic and challenging class that at the root of the most difficult behaviours, and at the heart of my most desperate students' attempts for attention was, most often than not, trauma of some kind.

Trauma was not a new topic for me. I had been living with it for years. But, for some reason even with the familiarity of it, I had not realized or fully considered how wide-spread the effects of trauma in a classroom full of kids could be. I was feeling somewhat overwhelmed by the requirements of a Masters degree, so I decided to front-load my research needs, and during the summer in between my GDE (Graduate Diploma in Education) and my Master's program, I dove into researching trauma from the perspective of schools. I wanted to learn how I could be better equipped to handle future trauma needs in the classroom so that as a classroom community we could again get back to more meaningful ways of learning.

What is trauma?

To better help us understand what trauma is, we can look at a simple explanation offered by Tom Brunzell: "Trauma has been described as an overwhelming experience that can forever alter one's belief that the world is good and safe" (Brunzell et al., 2015, p.3).

There are many different types of trauma. On a website called "Your Experiences Matter," sponsored by the government of Nova Scotia, Canada and the Nova Scotia Health Authority, it is explained that trauma can be categorized into six categories:

- **Single event or acute trauma:** a traumatic experience that has an overwhelming effect (ie: the death of a loved one)
- **Repetitive trauma:** traumatic events that happen repeatedly (i.e. being bullied)
- **Complex or compounded trauma:** traumatic events that happen repeatedly usually within the context of a close relationship (ie, physical or sexual abuse in the family)
- **Developmental trauma:** traumatic events that happen repeatedly and affect a child's development (i.e. neglect, or frequent hospitalizations)
- **Vicarious trauma:** exposure to another person's trauma, which then leads to the exposed person developing trauma symptoms (ie. parenting, taking care of, or counselling a traumatized person)
- **Historical or intergenerational trauma:** the effects of trauma are passed on from one generation to the next (ie. trauma experienced in residential schools) http://yourexperiencesmatter.com/learning/trauma-stress/types-of-trauma/

Healing from any kind of trauma can be a long and complicated process.

A quote that spoke to me was one given by Shawn Ginwright. "The greatest casualty of trauma is not only depression and emotional scars, but also the loss of the ability to dream and imagine another way of living" (Ginwright, 2018, p.10). I know from my own lived experience and from watching my kids and my students, trauma paralyses you! When it is left to fester, it is something that takes over your life and prevents you from living.

"Trauma is not just a mental health problem. It is an educational problem that, left unaddressed, derails the academic achievement of thousands of children" (Craig, 2016, p. viii).

We can not afford to continue to ignore what trauma is doing in our schools and communities.

How trauma affects the body

Trauma disorganizes the neural activity in a person's body and releases abnormal types and amounts of neurochemicals into the brain. It has been scientifically proven that there are biological and chemical changes in a person's body after they have been traumatized. These changes affect the way a child responds to the world around them. The child's behaviour may seem impulsive. That impulsivity is controlled by the neurochemical reactions happening in the child's brain (Howard, 2013, chapter 3).

A child may also respond through the four F's: fight, flight, freeze, or fawn. All four of these responses are the body's way to react to fear. In a *fight* response, a child perceives that they are in danger and becomes aggressive. A child in *fight* might glare at others or feel like kicking or punching something or someone. In *flight*, a child feels that their only option is to flee. When a child is in flight, they might have restless legs, their eyes might be dilated and darting around, or they might become increasingly fidgety. In *freeze*, a person knows they are in danger but are unable to flee or fight and instead they start to feel numb. A child will feel cold and have a sense of dread in them. In *fawn*, a person accepts that their situation must be tolerated as no other option has worked in the past, and their only option is to submit to their fears. Often children from abusive homes end up fawning as they have had no other way to deal with their realities (Kirby, 2018).

On top of all of the chemical imbalances, a traumatized child can also be oversensitive to stimuli. Trauma, as we know it, is not always stored as a narrative memory, but rather as something that is trapped in the senses. So, it is very possible that a child's trauma is triggered in multiple ways through everyday regular things. This is why children can be so reactive and so easily dysregulated. Things that an adult doesn't even think to look for—like the brightness of fluorescent lights, the smell of a specific cologne, the colour of a hospital gown, or a specific time of day or year—can all affect the sensory response. Trauma memories are stored in your body, and your body is constantly reacting to the sensory experiences that you come into contact with (McClelland and Gilyard, 2019). The reason why it is so important to make note of this is that "children's success in important environments such as school and relationships with adults and peers is highly dependent on their ability to stay regulated throughout their day... The dysregulated child is disruptive, time-consuming and unpredictable" (Chatwin, 2018, p.13). A simple classroom environment can trigger a child in so many unpredictable ways.

How trauma affects a child's behaviour and ability to learn

As mentioned before with all of these chemical and neurological changes in a child's body, a child's behaviour is greatly affected. When behaviour is not managed, all of us as teachers know it becomes impossible for children to learn. As discussed by Craig (2016):

"A deep-seated distrust of adults, coupled with hypersensitivity to perceptions of danger or threat, seriously compromise children's ability to learn. Instead of integrating new information or experience, their attention is directed to survival and defending themselves against reoccurring trauma symptoms such as heightened arousal or disassociation" (p.20).

When these behaviour problems start becoming an issue, the child may then avoid or try to control what is happening in the classroom. This avoidance and control can also lead to children developing headaches or stomach aches in response to the emotions they feel (Craig, p.20).

What makes everything even more complicated for the child in these heightened moments of arousal is that it becomes increasingly difficult for the child to know or express what they are feeling. The child is most often unable to make sense of or control his or her reactions. This is often when a child's behaviour is even more misunderstood, and a silent or anxious response can be taken to mean defiance. In reality, the child is most likely just trying to cope with stress the best they can (Craig, p.50).

As teachers, when behaviours happen, we focus on trying to bring order within the chaos. In desperate times, we may even offer rewards or threaten with punishments. However, "for a traumatized child a reward can be interpreted as manipulation and a threat as only cruel, both of which will only heighten the child's feelings around the situation" (Howard, 2013, p.49).

So what are the answers? Could traumatized children be helped through lessons in self-regulation to help reduce their heightened sense of arousal? The whole mindfulness movement seems to be saying that it could. Unfortunately, as Chatwin (2018) states, "this effort is misguided." Chatwin explains how a child from a trauma background can "only learn self-regulation strategies after they have been soothed effectively by a responsive caregiver… and have experiences of co-regulation" (p. 14). Practising co-regulation in a classroom setting one-on-one with a teacher is seldom possible, so we need to look for different answers.

This brings us to consider the need to find replacement behaviours. These are behaviours that meet the needs of the child, but are "less disruptive and more socially appropriate." Chatwin suggests that teachers need to look at the inappropriate behaviour (the heightened arousal, the disassociation, the silence, or the hypersensitivity) and determine what the need is behind this behaviour (such as safety, movement, sensory input, sensory avoidance, attention, comfort, or acceptance). Once that need has been figured out, then the teacher can find ways to meet this need, helping the child to move into more appropriate behaviour patterns.

In summary, what Chatwin recommends is for teachers to focus on three key components when helping children manage their behaviours in the classroom:

1. empathize with the child and acknowledge their pain
2. set limits to their behaviour and take the time to discover what the underlying needs

for these behaviours are, then find more acceptable replacement behaviours

3. offer students a choice, so that they can gain a sense of control over their lives (Chatwin 23-29).

As we are beginning to better understand how we can help children with trauma histories, the process may seem daunting and rather complex. The truth is that damage caused by trauma is not easy to heal. We also have to acknowledge that "many teachers are in daily contact with large numbers of traumatized children, yet they have little or no access to the types of supports taken for granted at mental health agencies" (Craig, 2016, p.99). This is also a sobering reality that can not be ignored.

Is there hope?

Helping students who have experienced trauma may seem like an overwhelming task. And yes, from having personally lived it, I can attest that it is on many levels completely overwhelming!

However, the more reading I did, and the more SEL (Social Emotional Learning) activities I tried in my own classroom, the more I discovered that there is hope. As Craig explains "healthy, stimulating school experiences can help children create compensatory strategies that allow them to reach their highest potential" (Craig, 21) and that "the brain's ability to benefit from enriching environmental experiences offers new hope for the thousands of children whose early life experiences are marred by adversity and trauma. **Schools can become healing environments**" (Craig 25, emphasis added). We have to keep believing that, or we won't be able to stay in this profession, as each year more and more students enter our care with complex histories.

How do we do this with the resources, time, and energy that we have? How do we protect ourselves from taking on more than we can handle? This leads me to another important conversation.

I read an interesting article during this past year that talked about a very important aspect of creating caring community. In "Moral Aspects of Therapeutic Education: a case study of life competence education in Swedish education," Sara Aldenmyr (2012) discusses the moral questions around whether students should be asked to share their deeper feelings with each other (as often is done in therapeutic classrooms, which essentially are classrooms that try to help students find healing from trauma) (Aldenmyr, 2012, p.25). This is a valid question, and it needs to be considered. My personal belief is that all questions given to students about how they feel about anything should be given in a way that makes it very clear that it is always their choice whether they choose to answer it or not.

Aldenmyr also brings up another important issue, which is that as teachers we are "not a parent, a friend or a counsellor" (p.32). I have spent a lot of time reflecting on this issue and have known early on that I needed to come to terms with what being a caring teacher meant to me. I also needed these good reminders to not overstep my boundaries (with lack of training or expertise in counselling) and to proceed with caution in my caring role. It *is* possible to get too burdened by a desire to help everyone, and if we don't share out that caregiving role, I know too well that it is possible to end up burning out.

Different authors seemed to have different opinions around this very issue. Maria Hayward, who studied the role of teachers in the lives of refugees, explains "although they are not counsellors, teachers are with their learners regularly, if not daily...and are also typically given the most esteem and trust by refugees among service providing professionals" (Hayward, 2017, p.165). This led me to believe that even without training in psychology, a teacher's role in therapeutic healing is important.

As I was in the midst of reading books and articles on the theory behind trauma and how it affects children, and as I spent time thinking about the concerns people have expressed with teachers as untrained counsellors taking these issues on, I stumbled across a few different articles that seemed to have a slightly different focus. These articles were talking about healing. One that made an impression on me was written by an author named Shawn Ginwright (2018). In his article, "The Future of Healing: Shifting from Trauma-Informed Care to Healing-Centered Engagement," Ginwright talks about how the current trend of focusing on trauma-informed care (as important as it is), from his perspective, was incomplete (Ginwright, p. 32).

This article was a real find for me, and a turning point in my understanding of my role as someone who was aspiring to be a therapeutic teacher. As Ginwright explains "the term trauma-informed care runs the risk of focusing on the treatment of pathology (trauma), rather than fostering the possibility (well-being)" (p. 3). This led me to believe that, also for myself, knowing about trauma was not enough and coping with trauma was not enough. Finding strategies for my students was not enough. At the end of the day, we don't want to just manage or cope. We need to find healing so that students can move on and not have to keep on living under the weight of trauma that they have often carried around with them for far too long. After reading this article, I noticed a change happening in me. I was starting to long for more information about healing. I knew what I had learned so far to be very valuable, and I didn't want to disregard any of the wisdom I had gained. On the contrary, I strongly believe that trauma-informed practices are incredibly important to implement in all classrooms. But something was missing from the perspective of a teacher who wanted to cultivate a community of care.

I decided, at this time, that I needed to follow my heart and to switch the attention of my research to a more healing-centred approach. I wanted to learn how to focus on "strengthening the roots of well-being" (Ginwright, p.4) for my students.

Inspired by everything that I now knew and had learned (and had studied over that summer), I jumped into my new year of teaching and started in a Masters of Educational Practice program. I was determined, more than ever before, to dig even deeper with my students, and to explore even further, how I could put into practice what I had learned.

Over the next six months, I continued to gather information, and slowly a picture of what healing in a classroom setting could look like started to form in my mind. I strongly believed and agreed with the writings I had found that said moving towards healing needed to be the goal of all trauma-informed care.

Where does healing come from and how do we move towards it? Through all the reading that I have done, the experiences that I have had in my personal life as well as my teaching life, I have concluded that healing can only happen in a community that genuinely cares. As much as the world increasingly tells us to find answers from within, or for us to become more and more self-sufficient, I have come to believe that all of us need each other, and we need community. I believe it is ultimately what we are meant to do with our lives: to live in community and to really care for one another.

Creating caring community in our schools might be one of the last ways for us to ensure that our students have a chance in moving forward. In today's world, all of our families are busy, and often they are fragmented; villages of community are torn apart or move away. Our lives are often lived very individually. As parents, we replace our time with technology, and young people quickly learn that the only way to find connection is through social media. We need to take back what it means to be human, and part of that is caring for those who are hurting. Heesoon Bai (2009) says, "healing has to be not only part of, but an important and central part of teaching today's world that is sustaining significant suffering and damage" (Bai et al., p.7).

It has been encouraging for me to hear that the very nature of a classroom community has the potential to indirectly be therapeutic (Hayward, 2017, p.178) and that a classroom can be a "powerful place for post-traumatic healing" (Brunzell, 2015, p.3). Brunzell goes on to explain how coming to school and being a part of a classroom is for many students the "most regular and predictable routine in their young life" (p.3). So, if we as teachers become invested in creating caring classroom communities that are accessible to all of our students, we can play a very important part in opening up opportunities for healing for thousands of children and youth.

It doesn't all have to be complicated either. Even though parts of this process require us to learn more, to gain new skills, and to become better listeners than ever before, it is encouraging to know that even simple things like noticing when a student is sad or withdrawn can have a therapeutic effect on them (Hayward, 2017, p.173).

As teachers, we are being asked to accept the privilege, the responsibility, and the incredible opportunity to become "front-line trauma healers" (Brunzell, 2015, p.4) for our students. Each one of us needs to decide: are we willing to invest our time into researching material, attending trauma workshops, really listening to students and their families, and being committed to learning how we can be transformed into this role?

The path towards healing

The deeper I descended into my inquiry, the clearer my understanding of what a caring community for my students needed to look like. As I started to formulate my ideas, a vision for a path to healing took place in my mind. I like to think of this path as one that requires each step to be taken in sequence, each step building on the firm foundation of the one before. Sometimes this path might even require us to take a step back and to revisit a stepping stone that needs more time. It is important to remember we can be in no rush, but rather, invite children to join us on this journey with time, the kind of time that a year living in community in school allows for. My vision, when I look at this simple diagram, includes people walking down the path together and no-one having to walk on it alone.

Stepping Stone One: Safety

Through my studies, I have concluded that the most important task, if we are to move students towards healing, is to increase our students' sense of safety. This is the baseline need for all of us. For any of us to be able to learn, to take in information, or even just to be able to let our guard down and to relax, we need to feel safe. Safe from harm, from ridicule, from dismissal, from threats, or from anything that might cause us to wonder whether our dignity will be upheld. As Chatwin (2018) explains, "Our target goal is fear-reduction to improve the child's sense of perceived safety" (p. 23). And as Crosby (2015) describes, we want to create "emotionally safe learning environments" (p. 225).

So how do we help students gain this sense of safety? Craig (2016), in her research on trauma, found that teachers who have consistent rules, who are predictable, and who create classroom rituals (p. 92) will help children feel secure. Another way to describe this could be teachers creating a wall of protection around their students. Allowing students to know what is happening in the day ahead as they look at the schedule (with changes already noted—things like an assembly or a visitor), assuring students that classroom rituals are in place and won't be rushed through, or by providing students predictable expectations on assignments and projects before-hand are just a few examples of how that wall might be built. At the same time, we must also remember that within those safe boundaries there needs to be flexibility and a way for the teacher to see and hear each student's needs daily and to make adjustments as needed.

Over the past few years, I was fortunate enough to be working in job share partnerships where predictable and structured environments were the goal. My one job share partner and I also experimented with starting a new ritual of having daily class meetings. It was a huge success, even though we acknowledged that we were giving up a lot of time to do that; however, because the students loved it so much, it quickly became something they asked for and expressed they never wanted to miss. In our meetings, we talked about chosen topics (such as: "What are you thankful for today?" "Is there anything on your mind that is bothering you and you'd like to share?" or "What makes you feel safe at school?") that were directed by the teachers. We also gave students opportunities to tell us what they wanted to discuss. Our students most often asked to talk about friendship issues or other issues that had happened at school.

Later on in the year, my students started asking me more specific questions about what I thought about them, what gifts I saw them having, or what words I would use to describe them. Soon a favourite activity was formed. The kids would sit in a circle and ask me to speak life and encouragement into their lives. This activity was often followed by my students wanting to share what attributes they also saw in me. This became a spirit-lifting and powerful experience for us all.

The depth of these conversations took us to relationships that were strong and built on trust and familiarity with each other. Our class meetings also quickly became a connection point for safety. They were a way for us, as teachers, to communicate to our students every day that all was well, that we had time in our day to just be together and to connect. We hoped that our students would know that they mattered to us as people and that we truly cared about them. Our daily class meetings were also a wonderful opportunity for us to build ritual into our day.

Students' thoughts about feeling safe or unsafe:

"I like my classroom because it is organised, fun, and there are many good ways to describe our classroom."
"Our classroom is a safe place. I always look forward to coming to school."
"I feel safe here, and people are really nice and from the start, I've made really good friends."
"Having trustful teachers and some classmates makes me feel safe."
"Friends make me feel safe because then you don't have to feel alone."
"My teachers make me feel safe."
"Being outside alone makes me feel unsafe."
"The time before and after school makes me feel unsafe."
"What makes me feel unsafe is when people bully me."
"Seeing people we don't know walking around the school makes me feel unsafe."
"I feel unsafe when I hear people talking mean things behind my back."
"Dogs running around without a leash makes me feel unsafe."

Students' thoughts about class meetings:

"Having family/class meetings actually helped our class to open up on things and to build our communication skills."
"I enjoyed class meetings the most because you can share fun and bad feelings, and others could help you."
"I enjoy class meetings because I love sharing about my weekend and how I am feeling."
"I enjoy class meetings because we just get to share what we are feeling and talk honestly to everyone."

Stepping Stone Two: Trust

"Children who experience attachment failures in their early relationship can learn to draw comfort and support from teachers and others they encounter later in childhood, provided their patterns of insecurity are recognized and responded to in a manner that repairs early damage." (Craig, 2016, p.30)

Trust. Such a quick thing to break, such a slow process to heal, and at times it seems almost impossible to regain. We sometimes wonder if someone who has had their trust broken will ever be able to trust again. Thankfully research tells us that through healthy relationships, a child who has experienced trauma can gain trust in others: first, with those closest to them (ideally those people being their family) and slowly, over time, with others too (Hayward, 2017, p.169; Craig, 2016, p.30). But it takes time—sometimes a lot of time. Trust grows slowly as students begin to realize that we as their teachers, and also the other students in the class, value them and see them as "whole persons who are of intrinsic significance and worth" (Metzoff, 1994, p.269).

While trying to build trust in our classroom communities, it is so key for us to focus on lessons in social-emotional learning which allow students to "create a shared environment and a shared history" (Metzoff, 267). As we all know, a shared history and shared experiences are the building blocks for all relationships. It is really difficult to trust strangers and people we feel we don't know.

Stepping Stone Three: Relationship

"Teachers must establish strong relational foundations in the classroom to ground the students in safety and belonging" (Brunzell, 2015, p.5).

Once safety has been established and trust has been gained, relationships will usually naturally follow. Hayward talks about the importance of two types of relationships in the classroom: that between the teacher and the student as well as that between the students themselves (Hayward, 2017, p. 177). It is important to note that often a positive teacher-student relationship can also be a springboard for positive relationships with peers. Once a student feels secure in their relationship with their teacher, they are then far more likely to find other "resilient relationships" for themselves (Craig, 2016, p.96).

Through all of the questionnaires that I gave to my students over the past few years, it became very clear to me that the number one issue on my students' minds was friendship. It became evident that when students talked about how they were doing in everything else (academic success, sports, their relationship with their teachers, homework, whatever it was), it was all secondary to the primary need of students longing to have friends. Students long to be noticed, to feel like they are accepted, and to feel like they have a place in our class community. I can understand that.

We are meant to be relational people, and in today's world finding and keeping those meaningful relationships is becoming increasingly more complicated. We text a few words and feel as if we've had a conversation. We post one picture and conclude we have shared everything we need to about our week-long vacation. We stick our kids in fully regulated and adult-directed activities and wonder why kids don't know how to play with each other on the playground. When did everything change? Where did the days go when we poured over each other's holiday photos on a couch together, sharing stories and laughing at memories? It seems like we seldom even talk on the phone anymore. Our students are craving connection. Real, live conversation and fellowship. When we lack those friendships in our lives, we quickly become very lonely, and the consequences of loneliness are real: "Our thinking and our brains suffer if we are lonely or feeling socially isolated...Feeling excluded or as if one does not belong has shown to impair reason and decision making" (Diamond, 2010, p.783).

Research points out that building positive communities within the classroom will quickly affect everything else that also needs to take place, important things like "academic learning and the overall wellbeing" that students feel in school (Howard, 2013, p.48). It is always a worthwhile investment to invest in these relationships and to ensure that they can keep on growing.

As we also know, friendships are sometimes challenging, and relationships take work. Another important aspect of building positive connections in our classrooms is to help our students work through friendship issues. This can be done by focusing on restorative practices. Some examples include teamwork, flexible seating, and community building activities (Craig, 2016, p.81). In my own practice, my job share partner and I decided to also make ourselves available. Because so much was being found out through our daily class meetings and through all of the sharing opportunities we had set up, our students were feeling more comfortable telling us about their struggles and asking us to help when problems arose. We chose to get involved and spent countless times trying to help students to listen to each other and to figure out ways to move forward together.

Students' thoughts about relationships:

"I do have friends. I am not lonely."
"People don't always get my jokes."
"I love this class."
"I get along with everyone."
"I don't talk to others that much."
"When I try to talk to someone, they never listen."
"I feel bad when someone has no one to play with."
"I get along with kids most of the time."
"My teachers not only care about me but everyone else too."
"Not everyone wants to be friends."
"It feels good at school because my classmates and teachers are honest."

"We say nice things and help each other."
"My classroom is a good place to be. Everyone includes me."
"I'm super shy."
"Only sometimes people ask me to play with them."
"I walk around alone sometimes."
"I thought it was good to know that other people could care for you."
"I know my teachers care about me because they don't ignore me when I'm talking."

Stepping Stone Four: Voice

"Caring involves stepping out of one's own framework of reference into the other, trying to understand what the other is saying, putting aside our assumptions, our agenda for the moment and really trying to hear what the other person is saying" (Noddings, 1984, p. 24).

Providing the space and opportunity for students to find their voice and to either share difficult stories from their life, if they so choose, or to daily share the emotions that they are feeling, is a critical step towards healing. Personally, I have only now, while writing out my story, come to realize how important this step is. It is not enough to occasionally provide this space for our students. Rather, permission for students to express their feelings should be built into everything we do.

It is understandable, however, that at first, this may be the step in the process towards healing that we, as teachers, are reluctant to take on. It is undoubtedly hard to hear other people's stories or the feelings that someone carries, especially if those stories and feelings are surrounded by memories of something that has caused pain. As Labadie (2018) explains: "As a teacher, it may be tempting to avoid discomfort in the classroom, but this is not realistic, nor does it honor students' lives. Many of my young students had already experienced death, grief and trauma. By acknowledging this and offering a safe space for them to share, the classroom became more inclusive and supportive" (p. 16).

An important aspect of the telling of our stories is the need that a storyteller has to tell the story on their terms and in their own time. As Schorcht and Wagamese (2008) say, "We're all storytellers. We always were. But most of us have forgotten that" (p.75). It's not that we don't have the gifts to tell our stories, but we need to make sure that the storytellers only use their gift when they feel the timing is right. A teacher, as the person who creates the space where stories can be shared, must also be sure that the needed time has been spent to establish a classroom community of safety, trust, and relationship before this invitation to share stories is made. Crosby (2015) talks about how providing "opportunities to make choices can give students a healing sense of ownership and control over their environment" (Crosby, 226). Sharing, or not sharing, their story is something that students need to have full control over.

Stories became a central part of my teaching. I placed special importance on sharing stories through books of hardship, struggle, bravery, and overcoming so that students could learn empathy and perhaps feel less alone. The grade level I was teaching gave many opportunities for me to tie these stories into the curriculum, often covering several competencies in one powerful novel or a deep discussion about an important topic. I wanted to also make sure that I was giving my students opportunities to process what they were hearing and for them to be able to express any strong feelings that were coming up for them.

As we worked through activities that talked about our emotions, about putting ourselves in other people's shoes, about scenarios that were difficult, or about friendship issues, I always invited my students to also do a written reflection about our activity. This way I could keep tabs on any students that might be struggling. I then regularly pulled kids aside or wrote them a note to make sure that they knew I was hearing what was being said.

When it came to discussing difficult topics such as slavery, residential schools, different forms of government, civil war, child soldiers and many, many others, I also knew that through these issues, it was important to make sure that students had a voice to express what they were feeling. Many classes, after rich and powerful conversations, ended with written reflective time to ensure that students were able to express their thoughts and any personal connections they were making. Carello (2015) talks about the importance of providing students with opportunities to "process, reorient, and regain emotional distance from difficult material" (p.270). I took this advice to heart.

In one of my classes, we gathered around the classroom carpet area daily and opened up room for check-ins and conversation. The carpet area became such a central part of our community. I found it so much easier to tackle all of these big issues with the students huddled around together in close proximity to me. I strongly sensed that the conversation was better heard and that gathering at the carpet to listen and discuss made our world a little bit smaller and safer. The carpet also became a place for the students to let their guard down, to participate in a conversation, to hang out with their friends, and to work together on assignments and projects. It was wonderful to hear from students how much they appreciated this simple addition to our intermediate room. This type of community is perhaps something we more readily find happening in the younger grades, but for some reason, we tend to turn away from these basics the older our students become. As Shahana Knight (2018) explains, small additions such as rugs, lamps and "the no shoes rules" can "allow children to relax... and encourage a readiness to learn" (Knight, p. 2).

Sharing our thoughts with others

"I love going to school. I like to sit at the carpet. I like that we have groups to work with people."
"I want to do the sharing circle again because we can share what we like and what we don't like."
"I really liked doing these activities because it gave us a chance to express our feelings."
"I liked making connections with others because I didn't know many of the connections that people had with me."
"My favourite activity was putting yourself in other people's shoes. It lets you know that other people know how you feel."
"I like it when we are in a circle talking about everything. Can we do it again?"

A shared story

I am starting to discover
the power of a shared story,
taking the risk to share in
vulnerability
and honesty,
even when the stakes are high
and it would be so much easier
to just keep on hiding,
to say nothing,
and to carry the weight of your story
alone.

But when we share that which is
uncomfortable
and hard,
we open a way for others
to see us,
to hear us,
to acknowledge
who we are,
the full sense of us,
not just the parts
that are seen
and heard
in every-day living,
but the explanation
as to the **why** behind
it all.

A story is also an invitation
and an opportunity
for healing
to begin to take place.

We listen.
We hear.
We open our hearts,
and we ask
to be changed
as the receiver
because perhaps now
we understand a little more;
and as the one who shares,
because perhaps now
there's hope that
we will be understood.
(K. Aldom)

Stepping Stone Five: Acknowledgement

"Imagine the small, clenched fist of a heart 'broken open' into largeness of life, into greater capacity to hold one's own and the world's pain and joy. This, too, happens every day. We know that heartbreak can become a source of compassion and grace because we have seen it happen with our own eyes and people enlarge their capacity for empathy and their ability to attend to the suffering of others" (Palmer, 2008, 6).

"After listening and reflecting, the carer must respond" (Noddings, 2012, p.72).

It was important to give students the opportunity to share their stories and to openly express their feelings. While we, as a class, listened to stories shared by our class members, it became vital to me that no one's story was left hanging in mid-air. So, during these times, with the writer's permission, we would continue to discuss themes that were found in a story, and I would ask if others had had similar experiences. My students were eager to share their own stories, and it was beautiful and powerful to see how these times helped bond our classes together and how students gathered around each other to encourage and to comfort one another if the story that was shared was one of a hard experience and had caused pain.

I always aimed to be extremely careful to make sure that prompts that were given during class times were about topics that would not get too large for us to process as a group. Some stories were complicated and personal, and when these stories were shared, it was acutely important to me that my students' privacy and dignity was upheld. I put into place safeguards, making sure I looked over all of my students' writing before I allowed them to share their story with the class. At times, what the students shared with me was too big for other children to safely process. When that was the case, I would quietly tell my student that what they had written was very important and emphasize how glad I was that they had shared it with me. But, I would also have to warn them that perhaps this story was one that the rest of the students would not know how to respond to in the best possible way because their story was incredibly sensitive. I would then explain to my student that I wanted to make sure they were protected. I would then go on to assure my student that we would find a way for them to share their story with someone safe so that they would not be left alone with it. It was during these times that I would then need to advocate for the right help to be found through counselling services offered at the school or by letting other staff members or parents know that a student needed more support. We adults would then find more private avenues for my students to process the specifics of their story.

A curriculum that allows for students to identify feelings along with their peers is a great way for students to continue exploring their emotions with their classmates, while still allowing privacy of the more intense details of some stories to be kept private. Integration of these types of lessons that identify feelings and give more generalized examples are a necessary supplement in a trauma-informed classroom.

One more important thing to note is that it wasn't just the hard stories that needed attention. It became evident to me that all of my students' shared stories needed a response. I wanted to find ways to respond to each student personally whether it was through writing or in conversation. So, I quickly learned how to create space in my teaching for that to happen. I wanted to ensure that students understood that all of their work and all of our conversations needed flexibility, where sometimes I had to say to my class: This is hard—we may have to get back to this later; I need time to look through everyone's writing and make sure that I am understanding what is being said; or I sense this is getting heavy, and I need time to ensure that everyone's thoughts are given the space they need. The students had to learn that our classroom environment needed to become a place where sometimes things would be revisited later and that we needed to make it a priority to create time and space to do that.

As Montabello (2008) says, "Working alongside others in this way requires a commitment to true listening, to recognize that the child, this teacher, this parent wants to say something important to me, something which I have to think about, something which may cause me to change my perspective on the child being spoken of" (Montabello, p.14). I knew I had a lot to learn from my students' stories, about their present and past, both of which helped me to understand what they were dealing with or carrying and how I could better help meet their needs.

The more stories we shared, the more clearly I saw that my students were looking for me to acknowledge and validate their lives and their feelings without judgement (Craig, 2016, p.13). As someone who is working through many types of trauma and a decade of complicated stories myself, I know that when people are suffering inside, it is crucial for their pain to be acknowledged for healing to start taking place. A very important piece to remember is that another person does not need to know the full story to be able to validate the feelings it has caused. This is something we as teachers also need to keep in mind.

Sometimes listening was all that was needed (Jennings, 2019, p.131). At other times, words of encouragement or acknowledgement needed to be spoken or shared in some form of writing. As my students and I entered this world of sharing stories, I wanted them all to know how important it was for all of us to not turn our backs on the storyteller. So, we practised together. We practised validating each other's words, acknowledging and encouraging one and other. We practised writing responses to each other that demonstrated that we heard what was being said. We practised communicating care for one and other and giving each other space to share our feelings in a warm and kind environment that lacked judgment or ridicule.

"More and more, in the alienated and frightening world we live in now, I think it is essential that we enter the dark places, and to face what is too painful, too hard, what costs too much. We have to look at what is in the distance, on the horizon. To listen to the language we don't understand. And to face the horrible thing in the locked room... We should ask ourselves again and again how we are connected to each other. And we should teach our children to do so, and not to turn away" (Lowry, 2015, p.24).

There is beauty in learning how to become vulnerable, as long as there are others walking along beside you, willing to show some empathy and willing to acknowledge your pain.

Stepping Stone Six: Purpose

Not for nothing

"In the same way I will not cause pain
without allowing something new to be born."
(Isaiah 66:9)

These words are the ones I cling to
As I try to answer your questions.
The ones of Why?
Why me?
Why again?
Why?
I have to trust.
I have to believe
this is not for nothing.
Something good can come out of
pain
loss
fear
suffering.
I have to believe it.
It's all I have to offer.
(K. Aldom)

One of my own kids asked me a question perhaps some of us have already considered at some point in our lives: "If God can do anything, why does He allow suffering?" I didn't answer right away, knowing how deep my child's pain at the time was. I did, however, gently offer a response: perhaps if we can find a purpose for our suffering, then we don't have to worry so much about the why behind it.

I have found several writings that examine the importance of finding purpose for our stories, and as our stories are often stories of pain, this leads me to conclude that the purpose must also apply to the pain. Battiste (2010) examines the correlation of our purpose in our journeys being tied into our gifts, and how our life journey is about us discovering what our gifts are (p. 14). If our journey includes a story of suffering and trauma, perhaps the journey of suffering can also direct us towards discovering those gifts.

I have been thinking a lot lately on how we tend to think of trauma as brokenness. But what if that brokenness was used alongside our gifts as a way to bring healing to others? As Brunzell (2015) says, "building mental health requires more than repairing illness...trauma-affected students need ever-present opportunities to build upon their strengths" (p. 6).

All students in our midst, need to start believing that they have something to offer, and that even though they may have experienced some really difficult things in their lives, when that experience is shared with others and used to help someone else, even that difficult experience can find purpose. As Craig (2016) explains, "When children experience themselves as a valuable member of their classroom community, they acquire new insights about their capacity to make positive changes in their lives" (Craig, 73). Teachers can be there to help students discover what their gifts are and why they are an important part of their community. In healing classrooms, "therapeutic teachers take the time and effort to get to know each student as a unique, capable person. They learn to recognize and celebrate each student's abilities" (Abrams, 2005, p.42). We need to find ways to recognize these gifts and to validate and acknowledge them so that students can be transformed (Jennings, 2019, p.88). All students have something to bring to the table, and our communities, by welcoming each and every student, can become more inclusive and diverse (Katz, 2012, p.7).

While trauma experiences often don't make any sense and leave us wishing they never would have happened, at the same time, experiencing trauma does offer us a way to relate to the pain of others and to care for them. Perhaps this is what humanness is all about. Responding, because we feel compassionate empathy towards others, the kind of empathy that results in action and moves us to find a way to care.

As I sit here at the end of March in 2020, putting the finishing touches into my book, I think about the world all around me amid the Covid-19 crisis, the amount of fear, suffering, pain, and trauma that people in every nook of the world are experiencing today. I once again start to reflect on the need for healing—healing for our students, healing for ourselves, our neighbours, our families, and our communities. We are going to need to find ways to care.

"You want to serve the world's needs — but because those needs are infinite, we burn out straining to meet more of them than is humanly possible. The fact that someone has a real need does not necessarily mean that I am called to meet it: I cannot give what I do not have. So, I need to know with real clarity what gift or resource has grown within me that is now ready to be harvested and shared." (Palmer, 2008, p.8)

During this past winter, I started grappling with the following question, "How invested do I become?" Somehow this answer seems clearer as a parent, because, of course as parents, we are fully invested in our kids and would do absolutely anything for them. As a teacher, how do I answer this question? It is no secret that "exposure to the information about the victimization of others results in emotional, cognitive and other symptoms...that echo aspects of the victim's experience" (Carello, 2015, p.263). So, how far do we as teachers go?

I once again return to the writings of Ginwright, where he acknowledges the need for others to gather around those who are providing healing centred environments (Ginwright, 2018, p.8). I don't think this can be stressed enough. Teachers need support, and so often they are not getting enough of it.

In today's classrooms, we as teachers are often left to deal with massive amounts of intense needs, and this makes our jobs very demanding. Even when we set up trauma-informed practices, and heavily invest into building caring communities, the truth is that "teachers who work with students with emotional and behavioural disorders know that their job is often challenging. High levels of stress and burnout are common among these teachers" (Abrams, 40).

The need for emotional and practical support for teachers who are dealing with traumatized children in their classrooms is emphasized by every author I have read. They all say the same thing. Being a teacher is a hard job, and it takes a whole school community being on the same page and caring about what is going on for it to be done well. Opportunities to talk about what is happening in our classrooms (Howard, 2013, p.57) and an honest and on-going support plan that is consistently followed through by administrators, support workers, and district level personnel (Crosby, 2015, p.228) is absolutely necessary. Any efforts put forth by teachers will not be successful without a compassionate and caring leadership team that is also making sure that their policies and practices are fully trauma-informed and focused on bringing dignity and healing to our children and youth. From what I hear, from what I have read, and from what I have also experienced, I am not convinced that these supports are being adequately provided for our front-line trauma healers in our schools.

This incredible responsibility and weight that teachers carry in their jobs is something that is often on my mind. In our GDE (Graduate Diploma of Education) program we were asked to reflect on several different capacities. We revisited these goals throughout our two years, looking for progress and growth in our development. I wonder what it would be like if a capacity of self-care or community-care of our colleagues was introduced? Would teachers finally feel that they were being permitted to also genuinely be cared for? Would it allow teachers to take better care of themselves as well as each other?

Where I find myself now

"I now know myself to be a person of weakness and strength, liability and giftedness, darkness and light. I now know that to be whole means to reject none of it but to embrace all of it." (Palmer, 2000, p. 70)

Who am I?

Who am I now
in this quiet house,
no noise to be heard,
those around me fast asleep.

Who am I now
as my body aches for rest
and sleep alludes me?
Night after night,
I lie fully awake.

Who am I now
as I try to make sense
of the life I've been given
and the roles I fill?
When the expectations I had and
the dreams I once dreamt are
perhaps slipping through my fingers.

Who am I?

A wife.
A mother.
An advocate.
A friend.
A sister.
A daughter.
A teacher?

In this new liminal space
of sleeplessness and silence,
I am waiting to find out
who am I going to be
(K. Aldom)

Letting go of good things

Letting go of good things
hurts and makes it hard to move on.
There's pain in the knowing
that good things have come to an end.

And yet,
how fortunate I am
when I am asked to let go
of good things, as
letting go
means I've had the opportunity to
hold something good
for a time.
And the good thing slowly
becomes a good memory
to enter into and to hold on to
for a little while longer.
And yet,

letting go of good things
hurts, and makes it hard to move on
because there's pain in the knowing
that a really good thing has come to an end.
(K. Aldom)

I was given an opportunity to write my own story and to begin the process of working through and releasing much of the emotion that I had been accumulating and hanging on to for the past decade. This process needed to happen for my own healing journey to begin. As of today, I don't know what tomorrow holds, as my family continues to live life and to struggle through many difficult situations and challenges, where we are waiting to be heard and understood. However I do know that over the past year, slowly I have come to realize that I too am looking for safety, for people to trust, for a place to make my voice known. I am searching to find people who will listen, walk along beside me, take pause and acknowledge the huge role that trauma has played and continues to play in our family's life. I am also slowly learning how to take better care of myself, to be vulnerable, and to allow for others to take care of me.

I continue to be hopeful that one day greater purpose for my story will also be found. Perhaps someone reading about my life and my experiences will feel less alone in their own experiences with trauma. Or perhaps my story will nudge someone to consider who in their life, whether professionally or personally, is needing someone to take pause, to check in, to inquire, and most of all to offer to be the one to walk beside and to provide much-needed care.

The Hallways of the Forgotten

Have you ever experienced time when
life itself becomes a distant memory?
It's been so long since
where you are and
what you do
has any part of the life
that those who know you
are living.
You go through the motions
knowing you need to exist in some form
or another, to somehow
be there and take care of
that which is before you,
but you are hidden somewhere
in the midst of
an existence that lurks
in the shadows.
And life as other people live it
is only a memory from
some distant past,
and instead,
you recognize that you are
walking in the hallways of the forgotten
trying to redeem that which was,
but may never be again.
(K. Aldom)

Shelter

Sitting here in silence,
bombarded by
the sounds around me,
a faint heartbeat
is the only reminder left that
I am still living,
and have not completely descended
into the land of the lost or dead.

Another morning of pretend,
struggling to shield everyone
from realizing how hard
it is to hold it all together
and to fake appearances
of things being alright.

All my energy is spent
withholding the tears
that sit on the edges
of my eyelids,
trying not to blink so that I can
keep them in sight unseen.
Striving my hardest
to hide desperation,
to tuck it away,
buried in camouflage
and to hang on to
that faint whisper
of hope,

holding back
resentment and frustration
and refusing those tears
of desperation to flow,
knowing once they begin,
there may be no end.

And then a pause.

A sweet song of truth
fills my soul and reaches
my ears.
Relief sweeps over me
even if just for a moment;
I linger, holding on,

embracing the reprieve as
I close my eyes,
trying to relish
this opportunity to escape.

I embrace
stillness...silence...faith
wanting to believe that
He is offering shelter.
I try to run. I try to sprint.
I want to get there.
I want to breathe,
but, once again,
I am stopped,
frozen, in mid-step,

pushed,
    back to reality.

Why am I here again?
The sounds of existence remind me,
and my pounding heart races
immediately into the deep
pits of fear
and anxiety.
No rest.
Not now.

The unknowns.
Not yet determined.
Reminders of
all that lies ahead
and the weary road
of trials
still needing to be
travelled and faced so that
somehow, we get there.

Oh, how I long to
find shelter for you
and for me

from this reality,
but once again it
is going to have
to wait
for another day.
(K. Aldom)

Trusting

Why am I having such a hard time trusting
that good things are meant for also me?
I listen to other's dreams,
Hopes, and wishes,
and my first thought is:
I'm sure you'll find a way
to make them come true;
I'm sure this is what will be given to you,
provided and secured.
We don't often share our dreams,
but I am reminded
it is good to have them.

And yet,
why is it,
that when it comes to mine,
I don't trust
that God would have my dreams
be ones
that have any place in my reality?

My fears are taking over my dreams;
my hope is fading.
I'm fighting a mighty battle
of believing,
and once again,
I find myself thinking that
everyone else seems to deserve

to have dreams
and to have their dreams filled,
but somehow deserving these things
does not apply to me.
(K. Aldom)

Words I longed to hear

I am here for you!
That must be so hard.
Can I come over?
I'm listening.
I want to understand.
Your friendship matters to me.
Help me understand.
No child should be treated this way.
We can do better.
We are truly sorry.
You are not alone!
I'll make room for you.
You're important.
How can we better support you?
What does your family need?
Your family matters to us.
We love you.
This must be so hard.
We believe you.
We regret the decisions
that were made in haste.
We are sorry.
We will accommodate.
I don't understand.
I don't have the answer…
…I wish I did.
I want to help.
How can I help?

Could I do this for you?
You don't have to be strong.
You are enough.
We are here for you.
This isn't right.
We will advocate for you.
Leave this to us.
You don't have to carry all of this.
We believe you.
This is not fair.
Your children matter.
This must be so hard.
I am so sorry.
You don't have to hold it all in.
I wish there was more I could do.
I don't have the words to say.
This is so unfair.
Why does one child
have to deal with so much?
It seems so unfair.
We'd like to get together—
what works for your family
right now?
This should have never happened.
We are sorry this
caused even more trauma.
You have the right to be angry.
It's ok to feel sad.
It is no wonder you feel this way.
We didn't listen.
Help us to do what is right

this time.
We haven't forgotten about you.
I will be there.
You don't have to say anything.
I want to understand.
It's ok to cry.
I feel so sad for you.
I'm here to walk with you.
We want you to know,
you are not alone.
(K. Aldom)

Will you be my person?

Will you be my person?
The one who
slows down, sets aside,
extends a hand,
walks beside,
and shows no judgement
because you understand
the need for safety,
the need for security,
and the need
for only real.

Can I take that risk
and have you be my person?
The one who gently reminds,
softly offers,
and steps into places
of unbelief and doubt
with a faith that covers
when your faith is not
strong enough to carry on?

Thank you for choosing to be
my person,
for not giving up on me,
for doing what is hard,
for hearing what is not easy,
and for caring when

it is only messy
and uncomfortable
and for now,
I am unable to offer
anything in return.
(K. Aldom)

Refuge

When you're living in darkness
and have lost all hope that
gentle light will ever reach your being again,

you're surrounded by a heavy
that leaves your whole body weighed down,
and you collapse under the load,
lying flat, unable to move.

You're surrounded by
so much that is hard
and you are crushed.
You try to move weary limbs
to reach out to something,
anything,
but all you grasp
is nothing.

God are you still here?
"for the Lord your God
will be with you wherever you go." [1]

Your voice cries out into
a space that sounds hollow

God, I need to hear from you.
"Call to me and I will answer you." [2]

Your thoughts wander
to things that once seemed so clear.
The candle that has been burning
from the time your life began
is dimming
and increasingly veiled in a heavy fog
that seems to be getting more
and more
dense as each hour passes.
"My eyes fail looking for your promise.
I say, 'When will you comfort me?'" [3]

God, please don't leave me here
again, alone
"And behold I am with you always" [4]

You can feel and hear
shallow breaths in your lungs
surrounded by
only
silence.

God, you have promised to walk with me.
"Surely your goodness and love will follow me
all the days of my life." [5]

But the candle is burning low,
and the flame is barely a flicker.

God, help me to hang on
until that day when the light burns brighter again.

And once again, you make a choice
to reach out one…more… time.
*"I will take refuge in the shadow of your wings
until the disaster has passed."* [6]

God,
help me to find refuge in you.
(K. Aldom)

All verses quoted from The Holy Bible. (NIV), 2011.
1) Joshua 1:9
2) Jeremiah 33:3
3) Psalm 119:82
4) Matthew 28:20
5) Psalm 23:6
6) Psalm 57:1

Healing

So very softly
the gentle warm wind
of healing
brushes over
with tenderness and
care.
A warm hand
delicately holds
the heart that
is bruised,
the soul that
is broken.
In a patient whisper,
soothing words are spoken
like a blanket
of safety,
providing
a nest of protection
against the raging storm.
(K. Aldom)

Let us take care of you now

My story was read,
and my story was told.
My words were
finally heard.

The deep sorrow,

the intense pain,

the hidden reality,
was finally revealed.

I released my truth.

I allowed myself to be seen,

and brick by brick
the walls came down.

"Let us take care of you now"
"Let us care for you"
"Let us care"
"Let us"
"Allow"

My sweet friends.
My wise caregivers.
Help has arrived.

I open the door.
I close my weary eyes.

And slowly, ever so slowly, healing
can now begin to enter in.
A deep breath, a sigh.
Help has arrived.
(K. Aldom)

References

Abrams, B. J. (2005). Becoming a therapeutic teacher for students with emotional and behavioral disorders. *Teaching exceptional children*, 38(2), 40-45. doi:10.1177/004005990503800205

Aldenmyr, S. I. (2012). Moral aspects of therapeutic education: a case study of life competence education in Swedish education. *Journal of Moral Education*, 41 (1), 23-37.

Bai, H., Scott, C. & Donald, B. (2009). Contemplative pedagogy and revitalization of teacher education. *Alberta Journal of Educational Research*, 55(3), 319-334.

Battiste, M. (2010). Nourishing the learning spirit: Living our way to new thinking. *Education Canada* 50(1), 14-18.

Brendtro, L. & Brokenleg, M. (2007). *Schools with spirit: nurturing the inner lives of children and teachers*. Lantieri, L. (Ed.). Boston: Beacon Press, 39-52.

Brunzell, T., Waters, L., & Stokes, H. (2015). Teaching with strengths in trauma-affected students: A new approach to healing and growth in the classroom. *American Journal of Orthopsychiatry, 85*(1), 3-9. doi:10.1037/ort0000048

Carello, J., & Butler, L. D. (2015). Practicing what we teach: Trauma-Informed educational practice. *Journal of Teaching in Social Work,* 35(3), 262-278. doi:10.1080/08841233.2015.1030059

Chatwin, A. (2018). *Teaching the hurt child: Relationships between trauma, attachment and learning*. A Child's Song Adoption Support Services.

Craig, S. E., & Stevens, J. E. (2016). *Trauma-sensitive schools: Learning communities transforming children's lives, K-5*. New York, NY: Teachers College Press.

Crosby, S. An ecological perspective on emerging trauma-informed teaching Practices. *Children & Schools*, Volume 37, Issue 4, 1 October 2015, 223–230. https://doi-org.proxy.lib.sfu.ca/10.1093/cs/cdv027

Diamond, A. (2010). The evidence for improving school outcomes by addressing the whole child and by addressing skills and attitudes, not just content. *Early Education and Development,* 21(5). 780-793.

Ginwright, S. (2018, May 31). The future of healing: Shifting from trauma-informed care to healing centered engagement. Retrieved from https://medium.com/@ginwright/the-future-of-healing-shifting-from-trauma-informed-care-to-healing-centered-engagement-634f557ce69c

Hanvey, L. (2002). *Children with disabilities and their families in Canada*. National Children's Alliance for the First National Roundtable on Children with Disabilities. Retrieved from: http://citeseerx.ist.psu.edu/viewdoc/download?doi=10.1.1.457.3999&rep=rep1&type=pdf

Hayward, M. (2017). Teaching as a primary therapeutic intervention for learners from refugee backgrounds. *Intercultural Education*, 28 (2), 165-181.

Howard, J. A. (2013). *Distressed or deliberately defiant?: Managing challenging student behaviour due to trauma and disorganised attachment*. Toowong, Queensland: Australian Academic Press.

Jennings, P. A., & Siegel, D. J. (2019). *The trauma-sensitive classroom: Building resilience with compassionate teaching*. New York: W.W. Norton & Company.

Katz, J. (2012). *Teaching to diversity: The three-block model of universal design for learning.* Winnipeg: Portage and Main Press.

Kirby, S. (2018, April 15). Fight flight freeze: How to recognize it and what to do when it happens. Retrieved from https://www.betterhelp.com/advice/trauma/fight-flight-freeze-how-to-recognize-it-and-what-to-do-when-it-happens/

Knight, S. A calming, therapeutic classroom environment | Headteacher (2018). Retrieved from https://www.magonlinelibrary.com/doi/full/10.12968/htup.2018.1.34

Kostelyk, S. (2018). *Self-Care for Foster and Adoptive Families*. San Bernandino, CA: Sharla Kostelyk.

Labadie, M. (2018). Second reaction: Stretching beyond the comfort zone: Using children's books as critical invitations to explore death, grief, and healing in the classrooms. *First Opinions – Second Reactions*, 11 (1), 15-17.

Lander, J. (2018, October 08). Secondary traumatic stress for educators: Understanding and mitigating the effects. Retrieved from https://www.kqed.org/mindshift/52281/secondary-traumatic-stress-for-educators-understanding-and-mitigating-the-effects

Lowry, L. (2015). *How everything turns away.* Speech presented at University of Richmond. Speech retrievable from: http://amytaramasso.com/authorstudy/pdfs/Richmond_Speech.pdf

McClelland, D., & Gilyard, C. (2019, August 27). Calming trauma: How understanding the brain can help. Retrieved from: Phoenix Society Burn Survivors https://www.phoenix-society.org/resources/calming-trauma

Meltzoff, N. (1994). Relationship, the fourth "R": The development of a classroom community. In Redding, S. (Ed.) and Thomas, L. (Ed.) *The Community of the School.* Lincoln: Academic Development Institute.

Montabello, S. (2008). *Journeying into the heart of schools: Dwelling in time, place and intimacy* [Scholarly project] Simon Fraser University.

Noddings, N. (2012). The caring relation in teaching. *Oxford Review of Education* 38(6), 771-781.

Paccard, G. (2018, March 17). Listen, understand and act: How to help someone burning out. Retrieved from https://medium.com/burnout-lets-reignite-the-flame/listen-understand-and-act-how-to-help-someone-burning-out-26126b38ab49

Palmer, P. (1993). Good talk about good teaching: Improving teaching through conversation and community. *Change* 25(6), 8-13.

Palmer, P. (2000). *Let your life speak: Listening to the voice of vocation*. San Francisco, CA: Jossey-Bass.

Palmer, P. J. (2003). Teaching with heart and soul: Reflections on spirituality in teacher education. *Journal of Teacher Education*, 54(5), 376-385.

Palmer. P. J. (2008). The broken-open heart. *Weavings: A Journal of the Christian Spiritual Life*, XXIV (No 2), 1-11.

Palmer, P. J. (2007). The heart of a teacher: Identity and integrity in teaching. In P. Palmer, *The courage to teach: Exploring the inner landscape of a teachers life*. San Francisco, CA: Jossey-Bass.

Purvis, K. B., Cross, D. R., & Sunshine, W. L. (2007). *The connected child: Bring hope and healing to your adoptive family*. New York: McGraw-Hill.

Schorcht, B. & Wagamese, R. (2008). Story words: An interview with Richard Wagamese. *Studies in American Indian Literatures, Series 2* 20(3). 74-91.

"Your Experiences Matter." Website sponsored by the Government of Nova Scotia, IWK Health Center, and the Nova Scotia Health Authority. http://yourexperiencesmatter.com

Zondervan NIV study Bible. (2002). Barker, K. L. (Ed.). Rev. ed. Grand Rapids, MI: Zondervan.

Bibliography

Abrams, B. J. (2005). Becoming a therapeutic teacher for students with emotional and behavioral disorders. *Teaching exceptional children*, 38(2), 40-45. doi:10.1177/004005990503800205

Aldenmyr, S. I. (2012). Moral aspects of therapeutic education: a case study of life competence education in Swedish education. *Journal of Moral Education*, 41 (1), 23-37.

Bai, H., Scott, C. & Donald, B. (2009). Contemplative pedagogy and revitalization of teacher education. *Alberta Journal of Educational Research*, 55(3), 319-334.

Battiste, M. (2010). Nourishing the learning spirit: Living our way to new thinking. *Education Canada* 50(1), 14-18.

Brendtro, L. & Brokenleg, M. (2007). *Schools with spirit: nurturing the inner lives of children and teachers*. Lantieri, L. (Ed.). Boston: Beacon Press, 39-52.

Brookfield, S., D. (1995). What it means to be a critically reflective teacher. *Becoming a critically reflective teacher* (28-48). San Francisco, CA Jossey-Bass.

Brunzell, T., Waters, L., & Stokes, H. (2015). Teaching with strengths in trauma-affected students: A new approach to healing and growth in the classroom. *American Journal of Orthopsychiatry, 85*(1), 3-9. doi:10.1037/ort0000048

Cajete, G. (1994). *Look to the mountain: An ecology of Indigenous education*. Durango, CO: Kivakí Press.

Carello, J., & Butler, L. D. (2015). Practicing what we teach: Trauma-Informed educational practice. *Journal of Teaching in Social Work,* 35(3), 262-278. doi:10.1080/08841233.2015.1030059

Chatwin, A. (2018). *Teaching the hurt child: Relationships between trauma, attachment and learning*. A Child's Song Adoption Support Services.

Child Welfare Information Gateway. (2014, November). *Parenting a child who has experienced trauma*. Retrieved from https://www.childwelfare.gov/pubs/factsheets/child-trauma/

Cohen, L. Holistic development and Inclusive education. Retrieved from http://acid.afid73.org/kaidd_abs/pds/20110600483_19th_A_7.pdf

Cole, A. L., Knowles, J. G., & Glenn, L. N. (2001). *The art of writing inquiry*. Halifax, N.S.: Backalong Books.

Craig, S. E., & Stevens, J. E. (2016). *Trauma-sensitive schools: Learning communities transforming children's lives, K-5*. New York, NY: Teachers College Press.

Crosby, S. An ecological perspective on emerging trauma-informed teaching Practices. *Children & Schools*, Volume 37, Issue 4, 1 October 2015, 223–230. https://doi-org.proxy.lib.sfu.ca/10.1093/cs/cdv027

Daneker, D. P. (2005). The body, mind and soul of trauma: Putting the pieces together. Retrieved from https://eric.ed.gov/?id=ED490603.

Diamond, A. (2010). The evidence for improving school outcomes by addressing the whole child and by addressing skills and attitudes, not just content. *Early Education and Development*, 21(5). 780-793.

Fels, L. & Belliveau, G. (2008). First flight into performative inquiry. In L. Fels & G. Belliveau, *Exploring curriculum: Performative inquiry, role drama, and learning* (pp. 15-37), Vancouver, BC: Pacific Education Press.

Ginwright, S. (2018, May 31). The future of healing: Shifting from trauma-informed care to healing centered engagement. Retrieved from https://medium.com/@ginwright/the-future-of-healing-shifting-from-trauma-informed-care-to-healing-centered-engagement-634f557ce69c

Goodson, I. & Deakin Crick, R. (2009). Curriculum as narrative: Tales from the children of the colonised. *The Curriculum Journal 20*(3). 225-236.

Gustafson, K. (2015, January 19). Teaching emotions: A different approach to ending school violence. Retrieved from https://www.yesmagazine.org/people-power/teaching-emotions-different-approach-ending-school-violence-sandy-hook

Greene, R. W. (2016). *Lost and found: Helping behaviorally challenging students (and, while you're at it, all the others)*. San Francisco, CA: Jossey-Bass.

Hanvey, L. (2002). *Children with disabilities and their families in Canada*. National Children's Alliance for the First National Roundtable on Children with Disabilities. Retrieved from: http://citeseerx.ist.psu.edu/viewdoc/download?doi=10.1.1.457.3999&rep=rep1&type= pdf

Hayward, M. (2017). Teaching as a primary therapeutic intervention for learners from refugee backgrounds. *Intercultural Education*, 28 (2), 165-181.

Hobson, D. (2001). Action and reflection: Narrative and journaling in teacher research. In G. Burnaford, J. Fischer & D. Hobson (Eds.), *Teachers doing research: The power of action through inquiry* (pp. 7-27). London, UK: Lawrence Erlbaum.

Howard, J. A. (2013). *Distressed or deliberately defiant?: Managing challenging student behaviour due to trauma and disorganised attachment*. Toowong, Queensland: Australian Academic Press.

Jennings, P. A., & Siegel, D. J. (2019). *The trauma-sensitive classroom: Building resilience with compassionate teaching*. New York: W.W. Norton & Company.

Katz, J. (2012). *Teaching to diversity: The three-block model of universal design for learning*. Winnipeg: Portage and Main Press.

Kirby, S. (2018, April 15). Fight flight freeze: How to recognize it and what to do when it happens. Retrieved from https://www.betterhelp.com/

advice/trauma/fight-flight-freeze-how-to-re cognize-it-and-what-to-do-when-it-happens/

Knight, S. A calming, therapeutic classroom environment | Headteacher (2018). Retrieved from https://www.magonlinelibrary.com/doi/full/10.12968/htup.2018.1.34

Kostelyk, S. (2018). *Self-Care for Foster and Adoptive Families*. San Bernandino, CA: Sharla Kostelyk.

Labadie, M. (2018). Second reaction: Stretching beyond the comfort zone: Using children's books as critical invitations to explore death, grief, and healing in the classrooms. *First Opinions – Second Reactions,* 11 (1), 15-17.

Lander, J. (2018, October 08). Secondary traumatic stress for educators: Understanding and mitigating the effects. Retrieved from https://www.kqed.org/mindshift/52281/secondar y-traumatic-stress-for-educators-understanding and-mitigating-the-effects

Leggo, C. (2004). Narrative inquiry: Honouring the complexity of the stories we live. *Brock Education Journal,* 14(1). doi:10.26522/brocked.v14i1.59

Lowry, L. (2015). *How everything turns away.* Speech presented at University of Richmond.

Speech retrievable from: http://amytaramasso.com/authorstudy/pdfs/Richmond_Speech.pdf

Lyons, N. (2010). *Handbook of reflection and reflective inquiry: Mapping a way of knowing for professional reflective inquiry.* New York: Springer.

McClelland, D., & Gilyard, C. (2019, August 27). Calming trauma: How understanding the brain can help. Retrieved from: Phoenix Society Burn Survivors https://www.phoenix-society.org/resources/calming-trauma

McInerney, M., & McKlindon, A. (n.d.). Unlocking the door to learning: Trauma-Informed classrooms & transformational schools. Retrieved from https://www.elc-pa.org/resource/unlocking-the-door-to-learning-trauma-informed-classrooms-and-transformational-schools/

Meltzoff, N. (1994). Relationship, the fourth "R": The development of a classroom community. In Redding, S. (Ed.) and Thomas, L. (Ed.)

The Community of the School. Lincoln: Academic Development Institute.

Miller, J. P. (2006). Ancient roots of holistic education. *Encounter, 19*(2), 55-59.

Miller, J. P. (1998). Making connections through holistic learning. *Educational Leadership,* 56 (4), 46-48.

Montabello, S. (2008). *Journeying into the heart of schools: Dwelling in time, place and intimacy* [Scholarly project] Simon Fraser University.

National Child Traumatic Stress Network. (2018, October 03). *Child Trauma Toolkit for Educators*. Retrieved from https://www.nctsn.org/resources/child-trauma-toolkit-educators

Noddings, N. (2012). The caring relation in teaching. *Oxford Review of Education* 38(6), 771-781.

Paccard, G. (2018, March 17). Listen, understand and act: How to help someone burning out. Retrieved from https://medium.com/burnout-lets-reignite-the-flame/listen-understand-and-act-how-to-help-someone-burning-out-26126b38ab49

Palmer, P. (1993). Good talk about good teaching: Improving teaching through conversation and community. *Change* 25(6), 8-13.

Palmer, P. (2000). *Let your life speak: Listening to the voice of vocation*. San Francisco, CA: Jossey-Bass.

Palmer, P. J. (2003). Teaching with heart and soul: Reflections on spirituality in teacher education. *Journal of Teacher Education*, 54(5), 376-385.

Palmer. P. J. (2008). The broken-open heart. *Weavings: A Journal of the Christian Spiritual Life*, XXIV (No 2), 1-11.

Palmer, P. J. (2007). The heart of a teacher: Identity and integrity in teaching. In P. Palmer, *The courage to teach: Exploring the inner landscape of a teachers life*. San Francisco, CA: Jossey-Bass.

Parenting a child who has experienced trauma. (2014, November). Retrieved from https://www.childwelfare.gov/pubs/factsheets/child-trauma/

Purvis, K. B., Cross, D. R., & Sunshine, W. L. (2007). *The connected child: Bring hope and healing to your adoptive family*. New York: McGraw-Hill.

Ross, E. W., Cornett, J. W., & McCutcheon, G. (1992). *Teacher personal theorizing: Connecting curriculum practice, theory, and research*. Albany: State University of New York Press.

Samaras, A. P. (2011). *Self-study teacher research: Improving your practice through collaborative inquiry*. Los Angeles: SAGE.

Schorcht, B. & Wagamese, R. (2008). Story words: An interview with Richard Wagamese. *Studies in American Indian Literatures, Series 2* 20(3). 74-91.

Shagoury Hubbard, R. & Miller Power, B. (2003). Triangulation and crystallization. Excerpt from *The art of classroom inquiry: A handbook for teacher-researchers* (pp. 124-133). Portsmouth, NH: Heinemann. [Chapter 4]

Stubenbort, K., Cohen, M. M., & Trybalski, V. (2007). The effectiveness of an attachment-focused treatment model in a therapeutic preschool for abused children. *Clinical Social Work Journal,* 38(1), 51-60.

Tanaka, M. (2015). Finding courage in the unknown: Transformative inquiry as Indigenist inquiry. *In Education* 21(2). 65-88.

Wilson, Jayne. Understanding separation, loss and the grief response (2005). Retrieved from: http://bcfosterparents.ca/wp-content/uploads/2013/03/Understanding- Separation.pdf.

Whitson, S. (2014, September 09). 8 ways to teach compassion to kids. Retrieved from https://www.huffingtonpost.com/signe-whitson/8-ways-to-teach-compassio_b_5568451.html

"Your Experiences Matter." Website sponsored by the Government of Nova Scotia, IWK Health Center, and the Nova Scotia Health Authority. http://yourexperiencesmatter.com

Zondervan NIV study Bible. (2002). Barker, K. L. (Ed.). Rev. ed. Grand Rapids, MI: Zondervan.

CPSIA information can be obtained
at www.ICGtesting.com
Printed in the USA
LVHW031946210720
661242LV00019B/1145

9 780228 833727